Stowe, Harriet Beecher

Uncle Tom's Cabin

Bloom's

GUIDES

Harriet Beecher Stowe's

Uncle Tom's Cabin

CURRENTLY AVAILABLE

The Adventures of Huckleberry Finn
All the Pretty Horses
Animal Farm
The Autobiography of Malcolm X
The Awakening
Beloved
Beowulf
Brave New World
The Canterbury Tales
The Catcher in the Rye
The Chosen
The Crucible
Cry, the Beloved Country
Death of a Salesman
Fahrenheit 451
Frankenstein
The Glass Menagerie
The Grapes of Wrath
Great Expectations
The Great Gatsby
Hamlet
The Handmaid's Tale
The House on Mango Street
I Know Why the Caged Bird Sings
The Iliad
Invisible Man
Jane Eyre
Lord of the Flies
Macbeth
Maggie: A Girl of the Streets
The Member of the Wedding
The Metamorphosis
Native Son
1984
The Odyssey
Oedipus Rex
Of Mice and Men
One Hundred Years of Solitude
Pride and Prejudice
Ragtime
The Red Badge of Courage
Romeo and Juliet
The Scarlet Letter
A Separate Peace
Slaughterhouse-Five
Snow Falling on Cedars
The Stranger
A Streetcar Named Desire
The Sun Also Rises
A Tale of Two Cities
The Things They Carried
To Kill a Mockingbird
Uncle Tom's Cabin
The Waste Land
Wuthering Heights

Bloom's GUIDES

Harriet Beecher Stowe's

Uncle Tom's Cabin

Edited & with an Introduction
by Harold Bloom

Bloom's Guides: Uncle Tom's Cabin

Bloom's Literary Criticism
An imprint of Infobase Publishing
132 West 31st Street
New York, NY 10001

Library of Congress Cataloging-in-Publication Data
Harriet Beecher Stowe's Uncle Tom's cabin / Harold Bloom, editor.
p. cm. — (Bloom's guides)
Includes bibliographical references (p. 89) and index.
ISBN 978-0-7910-9789-2
1. Stowe, Harriet Beecher, 1811–1896. Uncle Tom's cabin. I. Bloom, Harold.
PS2954.U6B55 2008
813'.3—dc22

2007043292

Bloom's Literary Criticism books are available at special discounts when purchased in bulk quantities for businesses, associations, institutions, or sales promotions. Please call our Special Sales Department in New York at (212) 967-8800 or (800) 322-8755.

You can find Bloom's Literary Criticism on the World Wide Web at http://www.chelseahouse.com

Contributing Editor: Portia Williams Weiskel

Cover design by Takeshi Takahashi

Printed in the United States of America

Bang EJB 10 9 8 7 6 5 4 3 2 1

This book is printed on acid-free paper.

Contents

Introduction

HAROLD BLOOM

Uncle Tom's Cabin; or, Life among the Lowly was published on March 20, 1852, and by about a year after its publication was reported to have sold more than 300,000 copies in the United States and well more than another two million throughout the world, both in the original and in translation. As Edmund Wilson noted, it lost almost all its popularity after the Civil War (which it had helped to cause), and did not regain a wide audience until the second half of our century. Wilson speculated that both sides, North and South, did not want to be reminded of the issue of black slavery for nearly a century after Emancipation. And yet, rereading it now, I have to agree with Wilson that it is a permanent and impressive work, forceful and fierce, a book worthy of the spirit of John Brown, who prophetically warned the nation: "Without the shedding of blood, there is no remission of sins." As a narrative, *Uncle Tom's Cabin* has its weaknesses, but the book is powerful in its characterizations. Wilson shrewdly said that the characters "express themselves a good deal better than the author expresses herself." I find this to be particularly true of Aunt Chloe and Uncle Tom, of Eliza and of George Harris and, most of all, of that magnificent and mythological monster, the superbly wicked Simon Legree, a plantation owner yet a New England Yankee, as Wilson reminded us.

Harriet Beecher Stowe, though moved by a biblical sense of urgency, was too shrewd to write her book as a mere polemic against the South. Her concerns, and her anguish, were patriotic but national, and *Uncle Tom's Cabin* indicts both North and South, in the name of Christianity. Because an "Uncle Tom" has become a black and liberal term of contempt, we need to begin reading the book by cleansing ourselves of our period prejudices. Uncle Tom is not only the novel's heroic protagonist but indeed is the only authentic Christian in Stowe's vision of her nation. A literary character greatly admired by Tolstoy and by Dickens deserves our careful regard. For Stowe, Uncle Tom is the Christlike martyr more truly crucified by the North than by the South, for New England had accepted the Fugitive Slave Act of 1850, and Simon Legree is, for Stowe, the diabolic incarnation of that hideous surrender of Yankee integrity. The last paragraph of the novel, still intense, peals out a prophecy worthy of John Brown himself:

> A day of grace is yet held out to us. Both North and South have been guilty before God; and the *Christian church* has a heavy account to answer. Not by combining together, to protect injustice and cruelty, and making a common capital of sin, is this Union to be saved,—but by repentance, justice and mercy; for, not surer is the eternal law by which the millstone sinks in the ocean, than that stronger law, by which injustice and cruelty shall bring on nations the wrath of Almighty God!

Some critics have remarked that Uncle Tom's Christian forbearance is unpersuasive to them, since it seems more than human. Perhaps the character is a touch more than human; there is a biblical grandeur to him that his utterances almost consistently earn. But he is more myth (in the positive sense) than cartoon or caricature, and the book's context sustains his martyrdom. Simon Legree doubtless is more persuasive: He owes something to the Puritan spirit in its decadence and decline, and he has his affinities to that other great devil, Hawthorne's Chillingworth in *The Scarlet Letter*. It is exactly accurate, aesthetically and spiritually, that his greatest hatred for Tom is caused by the slave's overwhelmingly sincere Christianity. The savage gusto of Stowe's villain was caught up splendidly in Vachel Lindsay's "Simon Legree—A Negro Sermon," the first of three poems that he dedicated to the memory of Booker T. Washington. Lindsay's chant concludes with a mad glee that Stowe might not have appreciated, and yet it testifies to the lasting imaginative power that had created Simon Legree:

And the Devil said to Simon Legree:
  "I like your style, so wicked and free.
  Come sit and share my throne with me,
  And let us bark and revel."
And there they sit and gnash their teeth,
And each one wears a hop-vine wreath.
They are matching pennies and shooting craps,
They are playing poker and taking naps.
And old Legree is fat and fine:
He eats the fire, he drinks the wine
Blood and burning turpentine—
Down, down with the Devil,
  Down, down with the Devil,
    Down, down with the Devil.

Biographical Sketch

Harriet Elizabeth Beecher was born in Litchfield, Connecticut, on June 14, 1811, the daughter of the Reverend Lyman and Roxana Beecher and sister of Henry Ward Beecher, the celebrated clergyman, author, and editor. She was subjected to a severe religious upbringing by her stern and tyrannical father. A follower of Jonathan Edwards, he preached hellfire and damnation in his thunderous lectures and scorned the female members of his family. Harriet, although remaining deeply religious throughout her life, developed a much milder and more beneficent Christian temperament. After her mother's death in 1816 she came under the influence of her eldest sister, Catherine, who a few years later set up a school in Hartford where Harriet was first a student and later a teacher.

Harriet began writing in the mid-1820s; among her earliest works are a theological essay and an unfinished blank-verse tragedy, *Cleon* (1825). In 1832 the family moved to Cincinnati, Ohio, where Lyman Beecher became president of the Lane Theological Seminary and Catherine Beecher founded a college for women, the Western Female Institute. Harriet was an assistant at the institute until the school closed in 1837. On January 6, 1836, Harriet married Calvin Ellis Stowe, a professor of biblical literature at her father's seminary. They would eventually have seven children; one died in the cholera epidemic of 1849 and another drowned in 1857. Harriet's first publications were stories written for the *Western Monthly Magazine* in 1833; initially her motives for writing were no loftier than to provide money for her family. In 1843 she published *The Mayflower; or, Sketches of Scenes and Characters among the Descendants of the Pilgrims.*

Harriet Beecher Stowe gained her first direct knowledge of slavery while living in Cincinnati. Kentucky, a slave state, lay across the Ohio River, and Ohioans were divided in their response to runaway slaves, some believing they should be returned to their owners. Both the Beechers and the Stowes were opposed to slavery and eventually joined the abolitionist cause. Harriet and Calvin Stowe once took in a little girl who claimed she was free. When her master came to claim her, the Stowes helped her escape at night.

In 1850 Stowe moved to Brunswick, Maine, where her husband had been appointed professor at Bowdoin College. There she wrote her antislavery novel *Uncle Tom's Cabin*, serialized in the *National Era* in 1851–1852 and published in book form in 1852. The novel was a tremendous success and was translated into at least twenty-three languages. It was, however, violently attacked in the slaveholding South (and also by some newspapers in the North), so in 1853 Stowe published *A Key to Uncle Tom's Cabin* to demonstrate the factual basis for her book. She followed *Uncle Tom's Cabin* with a second antislavery novel, *Dred: A Tale of the Great Dismal Swamp* (1856), based in part on the Nat Turner slave uprising in 1831; but it was poorly received. As a means of escaping from the vilification she was suffering in the press, Stowe visited Europe in 1853, 1856, and 1859. Her travel impressions were written up in *Sunny Memories of Foreign Lands* (1854).

Uncle Tom's Cabin and the Civil War made Harriet Beecher Stowe a celebrity and her name a household word. When she called on Abraham Lincoln at the White House, he greeted her by saying, "So this is the little lady who made this big war." John William DeForest, writing in *The Nation* in 1868, first used the phrase "The Great American Novel" to describe *Uncle Tom's Cabin*. Stowe, however, did not participate much in the Civil War, although her son Frederick William volunteered on the Union side and was seriously injured at Gettysburg. After the war she wrote a number of sketches of "leading patriots of the day" (all representatives of the Union cause, and including Abraham Lincoln, Frederick Douglass, and her brother Henry Ward Beecher), published as *Men of Our Times* (1868). She also turned her attention to journalism, contributing frequently to the newly founded *Atlantic Monthly*. The association was profitable for Stowe and the magazine, until the publication in 1869 of Stowe's "The True Story of Lady Byron's Life," a sympathetic representation of Lady Byron's separation from the poet and their marital difficulties, including Byron's incestuous relationship with his half-sister. The story lost the magazine 15,000 subscribers and dealt a heavy blow to Stowe's national prestige. Undeterred, she expanded the article to book length and published it as *Lady Byron Vindicated* in 1870.

In 1852 the Stowes moved to Andover, Massachusetts. After Calvin Stowe's retirement in 1864 from the theological seminary there, the family moved to Hartford, Connecticut. Stowe's novels of this period are chronicles of New England life: *The Minister's Wooing* (1859), *The Pearl of Orr's Island* (1862), *Oldtown Folks* (1869), and *Poganuc People* (1878). From 1868 to 1884 the Stowes spent the winter in Florida, where Harriet assisted in the cause of Reconstruction. Her descriptive sketches of Florida were collected as *Palmetto-Leaves* (1873). She also wrote a number of stories for children (*Queer Little People*, 1867; *Little Pussy Willow*, 1870) and domestic novels (*My Wife and I*, 1871; *Pink and White Tyranny*, 1871; *We and Our Neighbors*, 1875), which elaborate on certain points raised in a treatise she wrote with her sister Catherine, *The American Woman's Home* (1869).

Stowe's neighbor for the last twenty years of her life was Mark Twain, who reported poignantly on her increasing physical and mental deterioration in her later years. Harriet Beecher Stowe died in Hartford on July 1, 1896.

The Story Behind the Story

In 1839 the well-known abolitionist Theodore Weld published *American Slavery As It Is*, a collection of essays by people—both black and white—who had been eyewitnesses to slavery's cruelty. Sarah Grimké, a daughter of a South Carolina slaveholder, contributed one of the essays to the collection. Her account described a dispute between two slaveholding neighbors about the authenticity of religious belief among the slaves. To demonstrate a point, one of the men orders a religious slave to deny Jesus under threat of death by flogging. The bet is lost; the slave chooses death over denial. Harriet Beecher Stowe reportedly kept Weld's book by her side and was haunted by Grimké's story. Biographers report (Scott, p. 3) Stowe's account of falling into a kind of trance years later in 1851 wherein she witnessed a flogging of a black man. The imagined scene was to become the climatic moment of *Uncle Tom's Cabin* which she began writing that very day.

The political context that informs Stowe's novel is the national crisis that led to the Compromise of 1850. The conflict was precipitated by an attempt to determine the status regarding slavery of the millions of acres of new territory acquired by the United States in its war with Mexico. The California gold rush had attracted a population sufficient to warrant statehood, and settlers wanted the territory to enter the Union as a free state. Southern slaveholders, wishing to join the gold rush and to use their slaves for the hard labor involved, insisted that California be admitted as a slave state. Through John C. Calhoun, the powerful proslavery senator from South Carolina, the slaveholders created a national crisis by threatening the South's secession. At the same time, Kentucky senator Henry Clay won passage of the Fugitive Slave Act (1850) in exchange for the abolition of slave auctions in Washington, D.C., a spectacle regarded by abolitionists as particularly offensive for the nation's capital.

Raised in an educated Northern family, Stowe was naturally aligned with the abolitionist movement, but the greater influence on her developing views was her devout Christianity, which would have made any notion of the inequality of individuals in the sight of God untenable. The Calvinist strain of Christianity—transmitted by Jonathan Edwards—emphasized the depravity of the human condition of which slavery was one manifestation. Those who God ordained to be saved emanated a certain radiance that signified their blessed inner state. The reader encounters this belief in the characters of Uncle Tom and Little Eva who, despite being persons without status in society—one, a slave, the other, a child—nonetheless possess an unassailable otherworldly power. Stowe was also influenced by the revival movement known as the Second Great Awakening (1797–1831). Its proponents believed that sinful America could redeem itself by abolishing slavery. For these reasons, Stowe, along with her family members, most Northerners, and abolitionists found the Fugitive Slave Act demoralizing and profoundly offensive. Not only did the act criminalize Christian charity, it enabled opportunistic businesses to spring up to kidnap runaway and legitimately freed slaves alike and return them for a fee. Stowe begins her novel with an account of Mrs. Shelby's anguish and Mr. Shelby's ethical dilemma over assisting the escape of Eliza and her son. The passions aroused in both North and South by these national issues created a readership ready for the publication of *Uncle Tom's Cabin* in 1852.

The first forty-three chapters of the novel appeared in serialized form in the *National Era* (1851–1852, earning Stowe $300), a weekly newspaper established by the American and Foreign Anti-Slavery Society in Washington, D.C. Its original title—*Uncle Tom's Cabin; or, The Man That Was A Thing*—was quickly changed to *Uncle Tom's Cabin; or, Life Among the Lowly*. No clear explanation for the change exists, but some students of Stowe and her times (see Belasco, *Approaches*, pp. 21–36) speculate that the serialized form popularized in England by Charles Dickens was most successful when reader interest was sustained by the introduction of multiple characters and subplots.

Popular response to *Uncle Tom's Cabin* was astounding. It was the first American novel to sell more than a million copies. When John P. Jewett and the Company of Boston first published it as a two-volume book, on March 20, 1852, it sold 3,000 copies on the first day, 7,000 in the first week, and 300,000 in the first year. Eight printing presses operating simultaneously were required to meet the demand. England was the first country to print its own edition (twenty-two in all), as the novel's fame spread. Within a decade it had been translated into dozens of languages including Finnish, Armenian, Javanese, even Welsh (interestingly, the latter cannot be said for the work of Dickens or Sir Walter Scott). This was an extraordinary feat for a female novelist writing with such memorable detail about slavery.

One key to understanding the novel's popularity and the extreme emotional responses it engendered is to become familiar with the calculated use of illustrations by its several publishers. The first illustrated title page showed a group of black people outside a log cabin in a simple woodcut strongly resembling the traditional cover page style of the ubiquitous religious tracts presented as nonfictional accounts of the truth of the Christian Gospel. The effect was to suggest the veracity of Stowe's descriptions of slavery's cruelties. Another cover (see Gutjahr, *Approaches*, pp. 77–92) initiated a salacious reading of the novel with a lurid depiction of George's half-naked sister being beaten for resisting the sexual advances of her white master.

Surprisingly, *Uncle Tom's Cabin* had little legislative effect on the slavery votes in the election of 1852 (Gossett, pp. 180–181), but the novel aroused such high passions that people of all backgrounds and positions were stirred to register their opinions. William Lloyd Garrison, one of the most prominent abolitionists of his time, included in his weekly antislavery newspaper commentary or notices about the novel every week for a year. Praise (some of it modulated) came from Dickens, Tolstoy, and George Sand, the latter forgiving, even loving, Stowe's writing defects because they served such a noble cause (Sand, "Review," Norton, pp. 459–463). An anonymous reviewer for the *Times* of London (September 3, 1852) debunked Stowe's unrealistic portraits of black virtue and called the redemptive episodes of the scoundrels Sambo and

Quimbo "absolute and audacious trash" ("Review," Norton, p. 481). The *Frederick Douglass Paper* featured praise for Stowe's aims and her novel. Southerners, particularly women, reacted in fury with their own novels defending slavery and the Southern way of life. Stowe was accused of making up details about slavery most likely to lead Northerners to more vigorous antislavery efforts. In 1853 she was forced to refute the accusations by publishing *A Key to Uncle Tom's Cabin*, which cited eyewitness accounts.

Examples of the "extreme response" to the novel ranged from censorship to physical violence and butchery. An enraged slaveholder was incited to sever the ear of a slave and send it to Stowe, a Southern bookstore owner selling the novel was banished from town, and students from a Southern university held book burnings (Jordan-Lake, pp. xv-xxvi). On the other hand, Congressman Henry Wallace was emotionally undone while reading the novel on a train and had to stop for an overnight in Springfield, Massachusetts, to keep his sobbing out of public view (Norton, p. viii). The novel's popularity made the antislavery platform into a commodity: a variety of Uncle Tom paraphernalia was manufactured for sale, including paintings, figurines, dolls, plates, and wallpaper (*Uncle Tom Mania*, pp. 1–17). Thoreau, not even a reader of the novels of his time, reportedly had possession of a figurine of Uncle Tom and Little Eva given to him by a slave he had helped free (Thoreau, *Journal 4*, p. 630).

One result of the proliferation of Uncle Tom–related imagery was the ongoing reconfiguration of Stowe's novel these items set in motion. Countless adaptations in books, plays, minstrel shows, and later in movies and comic strips became confused in the public mind with the book itself and contributed to its temporary disappearance from the American literary scene. Other factors that helped to push the novel out of public view include the conclusion of the Civil War and the formal end of slavery, as well as a growing critical assessment of the novel labeling the work as too sentimental and popular for serious consideration.

In response to a letter from a curious abolitionist, Stowe wrote about the death of her beloved youngest son:

> It was at his dying bed and at his grave that I learned what a poor slave mother may feel when her child is torn away from her. In those [immeasurable] depths of sorrow . . . it was my only prayer to God that such anguish . . . not be suffered in vain . . . [and] that this crushing of my own heart might enable me to work out some great good to others.
> (Norton, p. 413)

Stowe had elevated the role of women in her novel, presenting domesticity as a blessed haven from the crassness of the industrial world. In her view, traditional women's work—the order and beauty of homemaking—was not drudgery. One of her aims in writing *Uncle Tom's Cabin* was to show how slavery disrupted households and the sacred ties that existed between parent and child, husband and wife. She went on:

> I write with my heart's blood. . . . This horror, this nightmare abomination! can it be my country! It lies like lead on my heart, it shadows my life with sorrow; the more so that I feel, as for my own brothers, for the South, and am pained by every horror I am obliged to write, as one who is forced by some awful oath to disclose in court some family disgrace. (p. 414)

Nothing written then or since casts doubt on the sincerity of these sentiments; but controversy arose quickly and persists to this day about her own views on racial equality and the effect her book would have and continue to have on race relations. There were also lingering concerns about whether her book was too manipulatively emotional to serve as a lasting document. In 1936 Margaret Mitchell wrote *Gone with the Wind* explicitly to portray a less negative view of the Civil War–era South. Black critic James Baldwin criticized Stowe in a long chapter in *Notes of a Native Son* (1955); her thoughts, he claimed, best belonged in a pamphlet not a novel because only a novel can take up the issues that mattered, namely the complicity of all human beings in acts of evil:

> . . . only within [the] web of ambiguity, paradox, this hunger, danger, darkness, can we find at once ourselves and the power that will free us from ourselves. (*Notes*, p. 11)

Following Baldwin, critic Edmund Wilson called attention to the need to reevaluate the novel:

> To expose oneself in maturity to *Uncle Tom* may . . . prove a startling experience. It is a much more impressive work than one has ever been allowed to suspect. (*Patriotic Gore: Studies in the Literature of the American Civil War*, New York: Farrar, Straus, and Giroux, 1962, p. 5)

The reassessment Wilson called for is under way. Revival of interest certainly was one of the effects of the civil rights movement that marked the mid-1950s to the late 1960s. Feminists interested in women writers brought Stowe back to life and offered psychological and cultural rereadings of her novel. In 1991 a San Francisco mime troupe produced *I Ain't Yo' Uncle* in which Stowe's characters put their creator on trial for the legacy of inaccurate representations of black life she initiated.

It would be impossible to list all the various manifestations of recent interest in *Uncle Tom's Cabin.* But without doubt one of the most interesting attempts to come to new terms with the novel is found in the recently published *The Annotated "Uncle Tom's Cabin,"* edited by Harvard historian Henry Louis Gates, Jr. and Hollis Robbins. The introduction considers yet another perspective on the treatment of domesticity and the objections made so forcefully by Baldwin. Gates makes for particularly fascinating reading when he recalls his understanding of Uncle Tom within the context of the Black Power movement. "Uncle Tom," he reminds us, had become a "such potent two-word brand of impotence that nobody really cared how far the public perception had traveled from the literary reality" (p. xi). In that era Uncle Tom functioned as the

> embodiment of "race betrayal" and an object of scorn, a scapegoat for all of our political self-doubts. He was

> the repository of our deepest anxieties about how our newfound opportunities created by affirmative action would affect our relationship with all those we might be leaving behind. We talked about him as *the* model to be avoided. (p. xi)

The reader may recall how Uncle Tom refuses to beat Lucy or to reveal to the odious Simon Legree any details of Cassy and Emmeline's escape plan. Like Stephen Dedalus in *Portrait of the Artist as a Young Man* who says to the face of national and religious authority "*Non serviam*" ("I will not serve"), Uncle Tom will not capitulate in the final scenes to his white master. Perhaps instead it will be the betrayers-of-race Sambo and Quimbo who will someday come to be associated with subservient and obsequious compliance in American culture.

List of Characters

Uncle Tom, a slave, is a figure of Christlike suffering and endurance. He is a loving husband and father, an honorable man in a dishonorable society. A model of passive resistance, he draws his strength from his unquestioning faith in the Christian promise of a better life to come. For Tom, the present is explicable only as a part of God's greater vision, so he patiently accepts the misery of his life and the lives of the slaves around him, without hope of social reform. His religious strength comforts those who suffer as it awakens in his oppressors a recognition of God's mercy and a fear of his retribution. He dies a martyr's death, refusing to betray two escaped slaves.

George and **Eliza**, although slaves on separate plantations, marry and have a son. The family stays together only through the clemency and the financial stability of their masters, and when Eliza learns that her son is to be sold, she flees north. George is reunited with the family, and they eventually establish a home in Canada. The desire for political dialogue and power ultimately motivates George to move his family to Liberia, a new African nation with modern ideals.

Evangeline St. Clare—"Little Eva"—is the precocious daughter of a slave owner. A kindred soul to Tom, she is a figure of spiritual purity. Like Tom, she believes that Christ will deliver all into a better life after death and that the task of both slaves and slave owners is to work to earn this reward. Eva dies of consumption, and her exemplary life motivates all who know her to emulate her kindness and compassion.

Augustine St. Clare is a slave owner whose beliefs are poised between the Northern and Southern viewpoints. He understands both the pretensions of abolitionist ideality and the cancerous corruption of slavery in the plantation system. He is kind and generous to his slaves and is both bemused and spiritually overwhelmed by his power over their lives. His self-confessed flaw is his laziness, and St. Clare's weakness of character costs his slaves their freedom and, in Tom's case, his life: St. Clare dies before implementing his promise to emancipate him.

Ophelia St. Clare is Augustine's cousin, brought from Vermont to oversee his household and the care of Eva. She is an organized, well-read, sensible abolitionist who is nonetheless repulsed by the thought of touching a "Negro." Through Eva's example of racially blind love, she experiences an epiphany at Eva's death that inspires in her a capacity to love her young charge, Topsy.

Marie St. Clare, the mother of Little Eva, is a self-absorbed hypochondriac incapable either of loving or of being loved, though Eva tries. She is irredeemably racist, and—by ignoring her husband's final wish to emancipate Tom—she proves instrumental in his doom.

Topsy, a slave girl, is the most startling and arguably the most charming character in the novel. Raised as though she were livestock, she has never known parents, family, or love, yet Topsy is as pure of heart as Little Eva. St. Clare purchases Topsy for Ophelia, challenging her to practice her Northern moral precepts and spiritual pretensions with a child who has known nothing of God or of family life. She is acutely aware of Ophelia's disgust at her touch and articulates her perceptions without equivocating. She and Little Eva become friends and, after Eva's death, Topsy's inherent goodness wins Ophelia's love.

Simon Legree is the corrupt and brutal plantation owner who buys Tom after the death of Augustine St. Clare. A spiritually barren man, he is ruled by his appetites and superstitions. Through him Stowe alludes to the sexual servitude of young slave women and girls in the figures of the tragically betrayed Cassy and the morally imperiled Emmeline. Legree beats Tom to death.

Cassy is the slave mistress of Simon Legree, sent to work the fields when he replaces her with Emmeline, a young girl purchased at auction. The daughter of a slave mother and a wealthy and loving slaveholder who meant to free her legally, the once-beautiful Cassy is refined and graceful. Alternately embraced by the white world and abandoned to slavery, she had lived a life of privilege with a white master in whose love she had trusted. But he abandoned her and their children, selling them all into slavery, and Cassy is filled with despair. She is drawn to Tom because of his spiritual strength. His stoic endurance restores Cassy's hope, and with Emmeline she escapes to Canada and is reunited with her long-lost daughter Eliza.

Summary and Analysis

In the short **preface** to *Uncle Tom's Cabin*, Harriet Beecher Stowe adopts a tendentious authorial voice that marks her novel as a call to reform. In abolitionist diction, highly moral and just as sentimental, Stowe advises the reader that "the object of these sketches is to awaken sympathy and feeling for the African race, as they exist among us," in pre–Civil War America. Slavery is the overarching evil to be eradicated, yet stereotypes of African Americans permeate the text from its first sentence, and the cultural superiority of the "dominant Anglo-Saxon race" is never in question. Through the experiences of various protagonists, the themes of the novel pivot upon a Christian model of suffering and redemption, the acts of the moral individual and the corresponding failure of a democratic society, and the troubling replacement of racist cruelty by racist benevolence. *Uncle Tom's Cabin* is a narrative of its time, but it offers to the modern critical reader insight into the pervasive effects of slavery upon American culture.

In **chapter one** we overhear two Kentucky men negotiating the sale of several slaves, including Uncle Tom and a four-year-old quadroon boy, Harry. Haley, the slave trader, and Mr. Shelby, their owner, are contrasts in appearance and caste. The former is a coarse, obviously prosperous man involved in a perfectly legal, if distasteful, business; the latter is a gentleman who calls himself "humane" and "hate[s] to take the boy from his mother," but must, after all, pay his debts. Haley reminds Mr. Shelby that a critical difference between slaves and "white folks" is that slaves cannot—and do not—expect to keep their wives and children. Stowe tells us that Kentucky has "the mildest form" of slavery and that the apparent ease and stability of slave life may deceive a visitor into believing that slavery is a benign "patriarchal institution."

Harry's mother, Eliza, overhears the slave trader's offer for her son and, astonished and distraught, appeals to her mistress. Mrs. Shelby knows nothing of her husband's financial difficulties, nor can she imagine that he would sell his slaves.

She assures Eliza that the sale of Harry is as unthinkable as that of her own children.

In **chapters two and three** Stowe depicts the dependence of the slave family upon those who own them. Eliza, the "petted and indulged favorite" of her mistress, is a gracious, refined, and beautiful mulatto married to George Harris, a mulatto slave on a nearby plantation. And although the couple had been married in the Shelbys' parlor, with "white gloves, and cake and wine," Eliza and George are at the mercy of the whims and indulgences of their owners. George is hired out by his master to work in a factory and invents an agricultural device, which earns him the admiration of his employer and the resentment of his master, who abruptly returns him to the "meanest drudgery" on the farm. Furious over his mistreatment, George reveals to his wife his plans to run away to Canada, where he will work, save money, and buy his family from Mr. Shelby. Unaware that their child has been sold, Eliza, who equates obedience to her master and mistress with Christian commitment, urges him to have faith and forbearance. George has less gentle thoughts, demanding, as if of God, "Who made this man my master?"

Stowe abruptly shifts scenes—as she does frequently in the novel—to Tom and his wife, Chloe, presiding over a humble and "respectable" domesticity within their own cabin on the Shelby plantation (**chapter four**). Tom's African features are "characterized by an expression of grave and steady good sense, united with much kindliness and benevolence." As Chloe cooks dinner he struggles to write, instructed by "Mas'r George," the Shelbys' thirteen-year-old son, and a love of home and of children pervades the slave cabin. Tom is a sort of local religious patriarch: After dinner, slaves arrive from surrounding plantations for worship and singing. At the same time, Mr. Shelby and the slave trader conclude their business in the master's house. Haley assures Shelby he will sell Tom into good hands.

Shelby's debts are cleared, and he informs his wife of the transaction (**chapter five**). She reacts strongly, urging her husband to make "a pecuniary sacrifice" to settle his debt rather than sell Tom and Harry, but he insists that "there is no choice between selling these two and selling everything." Mrs. Shelby resolves to see the slaves in person rather than arrange to be away when they are taken, as her husband suggests.

Eliza overhears the Shelbys' conversation and prepares to run away with her child. She stops at Tom's cabin to tell him that he has been sold and will be taken in the morning. Tom realizes that his value as a slave will be sufficient to save others from being sold and that by running he would doom them all. Eliza asks Tom and Chloe to tell her husband that she will try to reach Canada and meet him there.

Chapter six opens the next morning when the Shelbys discover that Eliza has run off with her child. Mr. Shelby, his honor at stake, rushes off to calm Haley and to offer his horses and servants for a search. With the complicity of Mrs. Shelby, the other slaves—in a rather comical interlude—conspire to hinder the search.

In **chapters seven and eight** maternal love is a powerful force strong enough to overcome desolation, cold, and fierce pursuit. In a scene that would become a literary symbol of female peril and endangerment, Eliza escapes across the Ohio River, literally one step ahead of the slave trader. Shoeless and bleeding, she clutches her child and jumps across huge chunks of broken ice. Throughout the novel slaves endure hardship and danger as a matter of course, but they must redeem themselves out of slavery by extraordinary acts of courage and spiritual strength.

A stranger helps Eliza up the Ohio bank and directs her to a nearby house where fugitive slaves are protected. A "poor, heathenish man," the stranger is impressed by her courage and exclaims that she has earned her liberty. Stowe dryly remarks that had the man been "better situated and more enlightened," he would have known not to assist an escaping slave.

Meanwhile Haley, having been forced to abandon his pursuit of Eliza, takes refuge in a nearby tavern. There he meets his former partner, Tom Loker, and Loker's new partner, Marks. He arranges for the men to catch the escaped mother and child. In payment, they will be "given" Eliza to sell in New Orleans.

In **chapter nine** the divergence of legislative and moral imperatives is evidenced in the passing of the Fugitive Slave

Act of 1850, under which the North was no longer a legal haven for runaways and Canada became the closest place of freedom. The reader is introduced to Senator Bird of Ohio, who defends the act to his unsympathetic wife, Mary, claiming that it will keep peace with Kentucky slave owners. Mary vows to break this law at the first opportunity. Although the senator admires her conviction, he makes a distinction between feelings and judgment when political unrest may be alleviated by legal compromise. But the appearance of Eliza and her child, needy and pathetic, appeals more strongly to his moral sense than an abstract, legalistic image of a runaway slave: "[H]is idea of a fugitive was only an idea of the letters that spell the word. . . . The magic of the real presence of distress . . . these [images] he had never tried." Eliza's journey continues as the senator secretly takes her to the home of a man who has freed all his own slaves and now protects others. Senator Bird gives the man money for Eliza and Harry's needs and leaves to resume his legislator's duties in Columbus.

We return to Tom's cabin on the Shelby plantation as he prepares for the arrival of the slave trader (**chapter ten**). Stowe invests Tom with a "gentle, domestic heart . . . characteristic of his unhappy race." He knows that this is the last time he will see his children, since few return from the southernmost plantations. Africans, whose "instinctive affections" are "peculiarly strong," whisper in terror among themselves about being "sold south." Escape to Canada requires that the slave overcome a "naturally patient, timid and unenterprising" character. Tom is an anomaly that Stowe defines carefully. Neither fearful nor timid, he is an archetypal passive resister whose eyes are always turned toward God. Honorable in all things, Tom will not ruin his master's credit with the slave trader by running away.

Haley leaves, having shackled Tom to prevent his escape. Young "Mas'r George" catches up to the wagon and vows to come after Tom and bring him back to Kentucky.

Chapter eleven opens in a small country hotel where a traveler, Mr. Wilson, comes across a handbill advertising a reward for the capture or killing of a runaway slave (George

Harris). The reader learns that Wilson is the manufacturer to whom George was hired out before his escape. Soon after, a stranger enters the inn and requests a room. Wilson recognizes the man, despite his disguise as a white gentleman of property, as George. Later, in George's quarters, Wilson urges him not to risk his life by breaking the laws of his country. "Sir," George replies, "I haven't any country. . . . But I'm going to have one . . . when I get to Canada, where the laws will own me and protect me, that shall be my country." Moved, Wilson offers George money and promises to deliver a token to Eliza when he returns home.

In **chapter twelve** the slave auction concludes, Haley takes Tom and his other human purchases onto a riverboat, and they begin a hellish journey south. Elegant white travelers comment upon the condition of the "Negro"; a clergyman manipulates Scripture to justify slavery; a mother tells her questioning child that although the separation of families is a "bad thing," it doesn't happen often enough to matter, and slaves are better off than they would be if free; a delicate and intelligent young minister predicts that God will bring Haley "into judgment"; a slave drowns herself after the sale of her infant son, and Haley records her death in his account book as a loss. The author interjects with the observation that "the enlightened, cultivated, intelligent" man is as much to blame for tolerating slavery as the trader for dealing in it.

In **chapter thirteen** we learn that Eliza and her child have found shelter in a Quaker settlement in Ohio and that the Quakers are making arrangements to secure their safe passage. While there, they are reunited with George, and they prepare to leave after sundown.

Tom's journey south continues, and he meets the spiritually precocious white child, Evangeline St. Clare (**chapter fourteen**). In the character of Little Eva, as she is called, Stowe concentrates a religious and moral clarity that the text suggests is possible only in children and in certain Africans. Eva and Tom become friends after he saves her from drowning, and her father, a Louisiana plantation owner, purchases Tom at her request. The story of Augustine St.

Clare and his family, continuing through chapter twenty-nine, describes the effects of a brutal system upon both masters and slaves. St. Clare is an impractical and tenderhearted skeptic, liberal and indulgent with his slaves, his hypochondriac wife, and his daughter. His forty-five-year-old cousin, Ophelia, travels with them from her home in Vermont to look after the delicate Eva and to help manage the household during his wife's frequent illnesses.

Ophelia St. Clare is "a living impersonation of order, method, and exactness." Well read and energetic, she is a firm believer in duty, religion, the abolition of slavery, and the proper training of children. Augustine, Ophelia, Eva, and Tom arrive at the plantation (**chapter fifteen**). Eva rhapsodizes on the beauty of her home, but to Ophelia it seems "old and heathenish." Tom is comfortable there. Eva greets "Mammy," a "decent mulatto woman," with repeated kisses, and the affection is returned without restraint. Ophelia remarks to Augustine that she could not kiss a slave as Eva does. In **chapter sixteen** Marie St. Clare, the languid image of decayed, effete Southern attitudes, counters Ophelia's criticism for separating Mammy from her husband and children when she married and moved from her father's plantation. "Don't you believe that the Lord made them of one blood with us?" Ophelia asks. "No, indeed, not I!" Marie replies, later elaborating, "And just as if Mammy could love her little dirty babies as I love Eva!" Augustine counters with his distinction between simple love for one's fellow man and the abstract benevolence of the Northern abolitionists: "You loathe them as you would a snake or a toad, yet you are indignant at their wrongs. You would not have them abused; but you don't want to have anything to do with them yourselves."

In **chapter seventeen** preparations continue at the Ohio Quaker settlement to help George and Eliza escape to Canada with their child. Once on their way, they are pursued by the traders Loker and Marks. Trapped with their Quaker guide in an isolated range of rocks, the former slaves defend themselves with George's pistols by firing on the party below. Loker is injured and deserted by his party; the fugitives continue their journey after leaving Loker in the care of nearby Quakers.

Like the suicide on the riverboat, another mother is destroyed by loss in **chapter eighteen**. Prue, who brings breads for sale to the St. Clare plantation, is a known drinker. She tells Tom that her life has been spent as a breeder of children who were all sold "as fast as they got big enough." She had hoped to keep the last one but, forbidden by her mistress to feed it, was unable to keep it alive. "I tuck to drinkin', to keep its crying out of my ears! I did,—and I will drink!" she tells Tom, as he tries to comfort her with promises of heaven. Since heaven is "where white folks is gwine," Prue prefers hell. In **chapter nineteen** she dies, locked in a cellar by her master. Ophelia confronts St. Clare about legal protections for the likes of Prue. He replies that there is no law to protect a slave and that the only "resource" is to ignore the excesses of barbarous people.

Chapter twenty introduces Topsy, a neglected, unloved, troublesome young slave girl. Dispensing with any natural attachment to parents or to God, she tells Ophelia, "I spect I grow'd. Don't think nobody never made me." Despite her constant professions of uncontrollable "wickedness," her inept thievery, and some pathological lying, we discover that Topsy is as pure of heart as Little Eva. Dark-skinned, with a "goblin-like" face and twinkling eyes, she retains a sense of self and a peculiar dignity, although her short life has been bereft of love. St. Clare purchased the girl for Ophelia to mold as she wishes, challenging his cousin to fulfill her Northern abolitionist ideals. Eva and Topsy become friends and playmates.

The scene then shifts to the Shelby plantation, where Tom's wife, Aunt Chloe, is hired out as a baker in Louisville (**chapter twenty-one**). The Shelbys agree to hold her wages toward buying back her husband.

In **chapter twenty-two** we see Tom and Eva again after two years have passed. By this time they have become nearly inseparable and Eva's health has deteriorated from "that soft, insidious disease" that we later learn is tuberculosis. She expresses her wish to free all of her family's slaves and to teach them to read and write, but this idea meets with ridicule from her mother. **Chapter twenty-three** introduces St. Clare's twin brother, Alfred, and his son, Henrique, who have arrived on a visit. Their unrelenting cruelty toward their slaves stands in sharp contrast to Eva's simple love of fellow man and St. Clare's ideal of true democracy.

Eva weakens rapidly and tells Tom and St. Clare that she is dying (**chapter twenty-four**). She implores her father to "go all round and try to persuade people to do right" about slavery, to "have all slaves made free." Eva tells her friend Topsy that Ophelia would love her if only she were good, to which Topsy simply replies, "No; she can't bar me, 'cause I'm a nigger" (**chapter twenty-five**). The ruthless clarity of the child's understanding cuts through the rhetoric of religious ideality and moral sentiment. St. Clare overhears the children and makes a Christian metaphor literal in order to translate Eva's message of love for Ophelia. He reminds his cousin that Christ had put his hands on the blind in order to give them sight. Ophelia admits that she is repulsed by Topsy's touch, yet she imagines, incorrectly, that the child is insensitive to it. "[H]ow can I help feeling so?" she asks. St. Clare speculates that Ophelia, an "old disciple," might learn from Eva, the younger one.

Eva's dying is a long and melodramatic process that evokes the pathos common in deaths by tuberculosis in nineteenth-century novels (**chapter twenty-six**). Her bedroom is filled with objects intended to bring only "heart soothing and beautiful thoughts," and she reads her Bible as much as her failing strength will allow. Topsy brings flowers, and the insufferable Marie cannot understand the affection between the children. Eva again tries, without success, to convince her mother that Topsy is not inherently wicked but has been unloved until now, and that the child wants to be good. Tom spends much time with Eva in her illness. They are kindred spirits, alike in religious faith and in imagination.

The effects of Eva's death are immediate upon the household members (**chapter twenty-seven**). As Topsy mourns the passing of the only person who has ever loved her, Ophelia is moved, at last, to love her young student. St. Clare wonders what he may do in response to the lesson of Little Eva's goodness. In his emptiness he turns to Tom and admits that he wants to believe the Bible but cannot. Tom says that he would give his life if it would make "Mas'r" a Christian.

Although religious faith eludes him, St. Clare becomes more practical and circumspect in the management of his slaves and informs Tom that he will emancipate him (**chapter twenty-eight**). Ophelia asks Augustine to make Topsy legally hers, and her cousin reminds her that she will then be a slaveholder and a "backsliding" abolitionist. But Ophelia understands that Topsy must have an owner to protect her and that by owning her she will then be able to bring her to the "free states" and give her liberty. But Topsy's emancipation papers are the only such papers St. Clare completes: He dies soon after, stabbed by a stranger. His master's habitual negligence dooms Tom, as Marie ignores her husband's desire to emancipate him and decides to sell all the slaves but Topsy (**chapter twenty-nine**). Ophelia writes to the Shelbys on Tom's behalf in an effort to save him from auction.

The scene in the slave warehouse, described in **chapter thirty**, is Stowe's most powerful and deftly drawn portrayal of the pervasiveness of the slave trade in America. Human property is valuable, so this New Orleans facility is a neatly kept house where slaves are fed and groomed for market "separately or in lots, to suit the convenience of the purchaser." Stowe carefully describes how the head of a "respectable" Northern firm, having become the creditor of a Southern plantation owner, is compelled to become involved in slave trade to recoup his losses: "He didn't like trading in slaves and souls of men . . . but, then, there were thirty thousand dollars in the case, and that was rather too much money to be lost for a principle."

A refined and "respectably dressed" mulatto woman and her fifteen-year-old quadroon daughter are among the lot to be sold with the St. Clare slaves. Susan and her daughter, Emmeline, have been brought up as Christians. The girl is expected to bring a high price for her beauty, and Stowe compares the mother's feelings to those of "any other Christian mother," except that she will find no refuge in religious or moral principle: The man who will receive the profits for the sale of the two women is a Northerner and a Christian. Susan is bought by a kindly man who tries to buy Emmeline as well, but he is outbid by Simon Legree, who also buys Tom.

The barbarousness with which female slaves in particular were "evaluated" and sold is also plainly evident in Stowe's slave auction scene. Although at the time any African ancestry legally designated one a "Negro," female slaves with traces of European ancestry were prized for their exotic beauty. The scene in which Legree, before the sale, runs his hands appraisingly over Emmeline's body would be outrageous and obscene to polite nineteenth-century readers—except that Emmeline is a slave of racially mixed blood.

Since the publication of *Uncle Tom's Cabin*, Simon Legree's name has, for good reason, become synonymous with evil and cunning. In **chapters thirty-one and thirty-two** Legree and the new slaves arrive at a place of cypress swamps, snakes, mournful wind, and rotting vegetation after a grueling boat trip upriver. Here slaves work without comfort and with only the meanest provisions and shelter. They rise at dawn to pick cotton; they eat at midnight. Still, Tom's faith in God remains unshakable, and in dreams Little Eva reads to him from the Bible. He works diligently in the fields and waits, with "religious patience," for some way of escape.

A strange woman joins the slaves at work in the fields in **chapter thirty-three**. Her delicate features and graceful bearing, good clothing, and scornful pride distinguish her among the ragged and hungry slaves as she picks cotton with fierce speed and skill. The woman, Cassy, initially does not speak but keeps close to Tom, as if sensing his singular strength. Tom helps a weakened woman unable to keep up with the fast pace of the work by filling her sack with his own cotton. Cassy muses that he will abandon all kindness once he realizes how hard it is to take care of himself in this place. "The Lord never visits these parts," she bitterly remarks.

Late in the evening the slaves return to a building where the cotton is weighed and collected by Simon Legree. He offers Tom a promotion to slave driver if he will flog the woman he had helped that day in the field. Tom refuses and Legree violently batters him, asking if the Bible does not order servants to obey their masters. "[M]y soul an't yours, Mas'r," Tom replies. Badly beaten, Tom lies alone in the refuse room of the gin-house, where Cassy comes to care for him (**chapter thirty-four**). As she tends his wounds and soothes his pain she urges him to give up hope in God. She tells him that she has lived, "body and soul," with Legree for five years and that now he has "a new one," whom the reader already knows as Emmeline. She argues against Tom's hope with the story of her own despair, but he maintains that Legree can really do no more to him than kill him and that Christ's promise of redemption will be fulfilled after death. The believer cannot lose, Tom contends, and Cassy wants desperately to believe. She tells Tom the story of her life as the pampered daughter of a slave owner who, like Augustine St. Clare, had meant to free her but had died suddenly before doing so. Cassy's sordid tale of the betrayal of love and the loss of her children is horribly fascinating—and is an increasingly familiar plight in the novel. Cassy is half-mad with despair, and Tom is her last hope.

In **chapter thirty-five** we witness the intensely superstitious nature of Simon Legree. Presented with a coin and a lock of hair found in a packet tied around Tom's neck when he was flogged, Legree thinks of his kindhearted mother, whom he abandoned to pursue the "boisterous, unruly, and tyrannical" ways of his father. Haunted by this reminder, he burns the lock of hair, which Tom received from Eva before her death, and hurls the coin through a window. Cassy warns Legree to leave Tom alone or he will lose time and money harvesting the cotton (**chapter thirty-six**). Legree, who attempts to force an apology out of Tom without success, vows to exact punishment after the harvest.

Chapter thirty-seven briefly returns to the story of George and Eliza Harris as they reach Canada. The exhilaration of their journey to freedom is mirrored in the renewed hope of liberty that Tom eventually inspires in Cassy. In **chapter thirty-eight**, Tom calms Cassy with his gentle and steadfast spirituality. He observes that, while he has the strength to endure his present servitude, Cassy no longer does. She plans a surprisingly simple escape for herself and Emmeline, whom she has befriended (**chapter thirty-nine**).

The garret of Legree's plantation house is believed haunted since the mysterious death of a slave woman there years ago. Cassy subtly revives and intensifies this belief in the imaginations of the slaves and Legree. So when she and Emmeline disappear, everyone believes that they have either escaped or have perished in the swamp, and the noises heard in the garret, where the two are actually hiding, only confirm belief in the ghosts. From her hiding place, Cassy witnesses the martyrdom of Tom (**chapter forty**). He refuses to reveal what he knows of the women's disappearance and is beaten severely by Legree and two slaves who have been made, by manipulation and abuse, to betray and torment their fellow slaves. The "savage men" repent, weeping and asking Tom to tell them about Jesus. Christlike, Tom forgives them.

In **chapter forty-one** young George Shelby, having received Ophelia's letter, at last locates Tom and intends to buy him back in fulfillment of his promise. He arrives too late to save him, but not too late to comfort his old friend at his death. Tom counsels forgiveness as he dies, and even Legree seems momentarily awed by his persistent faith and his saintliness. George vows to God that he will do everything he can to "drive out this curse of slavery." That night Cassy and Emmeline leave the plantation, and slaves will later speak of having seen two white figures "gliding" upon the road (**chapter forty-two**). Disguised as a Creole woman and her servant, they board a riverboat headed north.

In the same chapter we learn of a string of coincidences uniting many of the novel's characters in familial relationships long severed by slavery. A woman on the boat reveals the existence of Cassy's long-lost daughter—who, we learn, is Eliza (**chapter forty-three**). The woman, whose master had freed her, married her, and left her a fortune upon his death, is George Harris's sister. All are reunited in Canada, where the Harris household becomes a place of education, refinement, and family love.

In **chapter forty-four** Chloe and the Shelbys learn of Tom's death from George Shelby. Now the master of his father's plantation, George frees all the slaves, promising them fair wages should they decide to stay on. He attributes his change of heart to the courageous life and brutal death of Tom.

As the extended family of George Harris makes plans to emigrate to Liberia, the reader senses the author's perplexity over the future of race relations in a Christian democracy that has yet to abolish slavery. Through the character of George, Stowe suggests that the hope for true freedom may be possible only in another country. "[W]hat can I do for [my enslaved brethren] here?" George asks, in a letter to a friend. "[L]et me go and form part of a nation, which shall have a voice in the councils of nations, and then we can speak." He continues:

> We ought to be free to . . . rise by our individual worth . . . and they who deny us this right are false to their own professed principles of human equality. . . . We have more than the rights of common men;—we have the claim of an injured race for reparation. But, then, *I do not want it*; I want a country, a nation, of my own.

In **chapter forty-five** Stowe asserts in her own voice that many of the characters and incidents in the novel are based on actual people and occurrences. She acknowledges the troubling responsibility that will arise with the end of slavery: "Does not every American Christian owe to the African race some effort at reparation for the wrongs that the American nation has brought upon them?" Skeptical that justice to former slaves is possible in a nation in which the slave trade is firmly entrenched, Stowe suggests that the best way to make amends is to assure that the emancipated slave is provided an education before returning to Africa. She concludes with a resounding call to "repentance, justice and mercy" on the part of both Northern and Southern Americans, invoking the "wrath of Almighty God" on those who will not heed this call to save the Union.

Despite its melodramatic style, *Uncle Tom's Cabin* is an immensely moving novel and a social document of American culture. Harriet Beecher Stowe struggles, not altogether unconsciously, against her own racism as she attacks, with passion, a truly evil institution. By appealing to sentiment, evoking an emotional identification with the slave, and counseling a more Christlike interpretation of Scripture, Stowe may convince the modern reader that, if slavery was not the issue that caused the Civil War, it should have been.

Critical Views

Solomon Northup Describes a Slave Auction

In the first place we were required to wash thoroughly, and those with beards to shave. We were then furnished with a new suit each, cheap, but clean. The men had hat, coat, shirt, pants and shoes; the women frocks of calico, and handkerchief to bind about their heads. We were now conducted into a large room in the front part of the building to which the yard was attached, in order to be properly trained, before the admission of customers. The men were arranged on one side of the room, the women at the other. The tallest was placed at the head of the row, then the next tallest, and so on in the order of their respective heights. Emily was at the foot of the line of women. Freeman [Theophilus Freeman, owner of the slave-pen] charged us to remember our places; exhorted us to appear smart and lively,—sometimes threatening, and again, holding out various inducements. During the day he exercised us in the art of "looking smart," and of moving to our places with exact precision.

After being fed, in the afternoon, we were again paraded and made to dance. Bob, a colored boy, who had some time belonged to Freeman, played on the violin. Standing near him, I made bold to inquire if he could play the "Virginia Reel." He answered he could not, and asked me if I could play. Replying in the affirmative, he handed me the violin. I struck up a tune, and finished it. Freeman ordered me to continue playing, and seemed well pleased, telling Bob that I far excelled him—a remark that seemed to grieve my musical companion very much.

Next day many customers called to examine Freeman's "new lot." The latter gentleman was very loquacious, dwelling at much length upon our several good points and qualities. He would make us hold up our heads, walk briskly back and forth, while customers would feel of our hands and arms and bodies, turn us about, ask us what we could do, make us open our mouths and show our teeth, precisely as a jockey examines a horse which he is about to barter for or purchase. Sometimes a man or woman was taken back to the small house in the yard, stripped, and inspected more minutely. Scars upon a slave's back were considered evidence of a rebellious or unruly spirit, and hurt his sale.

An old gentleman, who said he wanted a coachman, appeared to take a fancy to me. From his conversation with Burch [Freeman's business associate], I learned he was a resident in the city. I very much desired that he would buy me, because I conceived it would not be difficult to make my escape from New Orleans on some northern vessel. Freeman asked him fifteen hundred dollars for me. The old gentleman insisted it was too much as times were very hard. Freeman, however, declared that I was sound of health, of a good constitution, and intelligent. He made it a point to enlarge upon my musical attainments. The old gentleman argued quite adroitly that there was nothing extraordinary about the Negro, and finally, to my regret, went out, saying he would call again. During the day, however, a number of sales were made. David and Caroline were purchased together by a Natchez planter. They left us, grinning broadly, and in a most happy state of mind, caused by the fact of their not being separated. Sethe was sold to a planter of Baton Rouge, her eyes flashing with anger as she was led away.

The same man also purchased Randall. The little fellow was made to jump, and run across the floor, and perform many other feats, exhibiting his activity and condition. All the time the trade was going on, Eliza was crying aloud, and wringing her hands. She besought the man not to buy him, unless he also bought herself and Emily. She promised, in that case, to be the most faithful slave that ever lived. The man answered that he could not afford it, and then Eliza burst into a paroxysm of grief, weeping plaintively. Freeman turned round to her, savagely, with his whip in his up-lifted hand, ordering her to stop her noise, or he would flog her. He would not have such work—such snivelling; and unless she ceased that minute, he would take her to the yard and give her a hundred lashes. Yes, he would take the nonsense out of her pretty quick—if he didn't, might he be d—d. Eliza shrunk before him, and tried to wipe away her tears, but it was all in vain. She wanted to be with her children, she said, the little time she had to live. All the frowns and threats of Freeman, could not wholly silence the afflicted mother. She kept on begging and beseeching them, most piteously, not to separate the three. Over and over again she told them how she loved her boy. A great many times she repeated her former promises—how very faithful and obedient she would be; how hard she would labor day and night, to the last moment of her life, if he would only buy them all together. But it was of no avail; the man could not afford it. The bargain was agreed upon, and Randall must go alone. Then Eliza ran to him; embraced him passionately; kissed him again and again; told him to remember her—all the while her tears falling in the boy's face like rain.

Freeman damned her, calling her a blubbering, bawling wench, and ordered her to go to her place, and behave herself, and be somebody. He swore he wouldn't stand such stuff but a little longer. He would soon give her something to cry about, if she was not mighty careful, and that she might depend upon.

Note

1. From *Twelve Years a Slave* (Auburn, Buffalo, London, 1853) 78ff; qtd. in Herbert Aptheker, ed., *A Documentary History of the Negro People in the United States* (New York: Citadel, 1969) 206–8.

William Wells Brown Describes a Kidnapping

I left Cadiz this morning at four o'clock, on my way for Mount Pleasant [Ohio]. Passing through Georgetown at about five o'clock, I found the citizens standing upon the corners of the streets, talking as though something had occurred during the night. Upon inquiry, I learned that about ten o'clock at night, five or six men went to the house of a colored man by the name of John Wilkinson, broke open the door, knocked down the man and his wife, and beat them severely, and seized their boy, aged fourteen years, and carried him off into Slavery. After the father of the boy had recovered himself, he raised the alarm, and with the aid of some of the neighbors, put out in pursuit of the kidnappers, and followed them to the river; but they were too late. The villains crossed the river, and passed into Virginia. I visited the afflicted family this morning. When I entered the house, I found the mother seated with her face buried in her hands, weeping for the loss of her child. The mother was much bruised, and the floor was covered in several places with blood. I had been in the house but a short time, when the father returned from the chase of the kidnappers. When he entered the house, and told the wife that their child was lost forever, the mother wrung her hands and screamed out, "Oh, my boy! oh, my boy! I want to see my child!" and raved as though she was a maniac. I was compelled to turn aside and weep for the first time since I came into the State. I would that every Northern apologist for Slavery, could have been present to have beheld that scene. I hope to God that it may never be my lot to behold another such. One of the villains was recognized, but it was by a colored man, and the colored people have not the right of their oath in this State. This villain will go unwhipped of Justice. What have the North to do with Slavery? Ever yours, for the slave.

Note

1. From a letter written by the ex-slave, abolitionist, and author William Wells Brown, dated September 27, 1844, to Sydney H. Gay, editor of the *National Anti-Slavery Standard*, where it appeared on November 7, 1844; rep, in Herbert Aptheker, ed., *A Documentary History of the Negro People in the United States* (New York: Citadel, 1969) 245–46. Copyright © 1969 by Herbert Aptheker. Published by arrangement with Carol Publishing Group.

An Anonymous Writer on Stowe's Depiction of Impossible Virtue

Uncle Tom is a paragon of virtue. He is more than mortal in his powers of endurance, in his devotion, in his self-denial, in his Christian profession and practice, and in his abhorrence of spirituous liquors. When Mr. Haley in his turn sold Tom to a new master, the good-natured owner informed his new acquisition that he would make him "coachy," on condition that he would not get drunk more than once a-week, unless in cases of emergency, whereupon "Tom looked surprised and rather hurt, and said, 'I never drink, Mas'r.'" This may be taken as a keynote to the tune Tom is eternally playing for our edification and moral improvement. He always "looks surprised and rather hurt" on such occasions. He is described as a fine, powerful negro, walking through the world with a Bible in his hands, and virtuous indignation on his lips, both ready to be called into requisition on the slightest provocation, in season and out of season, at work or at play, by your leave or without it, in sorrow or in joy, for the benefit of his superiors or for the castigation of his equals. A prominent fault of this production is indicated in these facts. In her very eagerness to accomplish her amiable intention, Mrs. Stowe ludicrously stumbles and falls very far short of her object. She should surely have contented herself with proving the infamy of the slave system, and not been tempted to establish the superiority of the African nature over that of the Anglo-Saxon and of every other known race. We have read some novels in our time, and occupied not a few precious hours in the proceedings of their heroines and heroes; but we can scarcely remember ever to have encountered either gentle knight or gentler dame to whom we could not easily have brought home the imputation of human frailty. The mark of the first fall has been there, though the hues might be of the faintest. . . . In [Uncle Tom] the said mark is eradicated once and forever. He represents in his person the only well-authenticated instance we know, in modern times, of that laudable principle, in virtue of which a man presents his left cheek to be smitten after his first has been slapped. The more you "larrup" Uncle Tom the more he blesses you; the greater his bodily agony the more intense becomes his spiritual delight. The more he ought to complain the more he doesn't; the less he has cause for taking a pleasant view of life and human dealings, the less he finds reason to repine; and his particular sentiments are all to match. Tom has reason to believe that Mr. Shelby will not wish him "Good by" before he starts off for the south with Mr. Haley. "That ar hurt me more than sellin', it did." Tom's wife is heartbroken at his departure, and naturally reproaches Mr. Shelby for turning him into money. Tom, always superior to human nature, tenderly rebukes her. . . . What have we been doing all these years, during which at great cost of time, labor, and money, we have despatched missionary after missionary to the heathen, but neglected needful labors at home in order to effect works of supererogation abroad? Before we export another white enthusiast from Exeter-hall, let us import a dozen or two blacks to teach Exeter-hall[1] its most obvious Christian duties. If Mrs. Stowe's portraiture is correct, and if Uncle Tom is a type of a class, we deliberately assert that we have nothing more to communicate to the negro, but everything to learn from his profession and practice. No wonder that Tom works miracles by his example. Such sudden conversions from brutality to humility, from glaring infidelity to the most childlike belief, as are presented to our admiration in these volumes, have never been wrought on earth since the days of the Apostles. One of the best sketches in the book is that of a little black imp, by name Topsy, who loves lying for the sake of lying, who is more mischievous than a monkey, and in all respects as ignorant; yet she has hardly had time to remove from her soul the rubbish accumulated there from her birth, and to prepare her mind for the reception of the most practical truths, before—without any sufficient reason—"a ray of real belief, a ray of heavenly love penetrates the darkness of her heathen soul," and enables her in due time to accept the responsible appointment of missionary to a station in Africa. Uncle Tom not only converts by his arguments Mr. St. Clare, his master in New Orleans, who is a gentleman, a scholar, a philosopher, and as shrewd a hand in a discussion as you are ever likely to encounter, but positively redeems in a moment from utter savageness and the lowest degradation wretches in whom the sense of feeling is extinct, and from whom we have been taught until Tom took them in hand to recoil in horror. . . . A quadroon slave called Cassy is introduced to the reader under the most painful circumstances. Her career has been one of compelled vice until her spirit has finally acquired a wild and positively fiendish character. You read the authoress' vivid descriptions, you note the creature's conduct, and you are convinced that it will take years to restore human tenderness to that bruised soul, to say nothing of belief in Heaven and its solemn and mysterious promises. But you err! In an instant, and most miraculously, "the long winter of despair, the ice of years gives way, and the dark despairing woman weeps and prays." She, too, "yields at once, and with her whole soul, to every good influence, and becomes a devout and tender Christian." This monstrous instance is outdone by another. Sambo and Quimbo are two black rascals, who have been trained "in savageness and brutality as systematically as bulldogs, and, by long practice in hardness and cruelty, have brought their whole nature to about the same range of capacities." When we first behold them, we are told to mark "their coarse, dark, heavy features; their great eyes rolling enviously on each other; their barbarous, guttural, half-brute intonation; their dilapidated garments fluttering in the wind," and to remember the apt illustration before us "of the fact that brutal men are lower even than animals." So long as these worthies are on the scene, their actions correspond exactly with their appearance, and with the accounts given of their canine bringing up; they go on from bad to worse, and at the worst, when their restitution to humanity seems utterly and forever hopeless, then it is that Tom "pours forth a few energetic sentences of that wondrous One—his life, his death, his everlasting presence and power to save,"—that "they weep—both the two savage men,"—that Tom cries to Heaven to give him two more souls, and that the prayer is immediately and satisfactorily answered by their happy and most astounding conversion. Surely there is something more real and substantial in Mrs. Stowe's volumes to account for their extraordinary popularity than such absolute and audacious trash. It would be blasphemy to believe in such revelations, and common sense and a feeling of what is due to our better nature will assuredly prevent all but the veriest fanatics from accepting as truth such exaggerated and unholy fables.

Note

1. The London headquarters of most of the philanthropic and reform societies in England [*Editor*].

James Baldwin on the Failure of the Protest Novel

In *Uncle Tom's Cabin*, that cornerstone of American social protest fiction, St. Clare, the kindly master, remarks to his coldly disapproving Yankee cousin, Miss Ophelia, that, so far as he is able to tell, the blacks have been turned over to the devil for the benefit of the whites in this world—however, he adds thoughtfully, it may turn out in the next. Miss Ophelia's reaction is, at least, vehemently right-minded: "This is perfectly horrible!" she exclaims. "You ought to be ashamed of yourselves!"

Miss Ophelia, as we may suppose, was speaking for the author; her exclamation is . . . moral, neatly framed, and incontestable. . . . She and St. Clare are terribly in earnest. Neither of them questions the medieval morality from which their dialogue springs: black, white, the devil, the next world—posing its alternatives between heaven and the flames—were realities for them as, of course, they were for their creator. They spurned and were terrified of the darkness, striving mightily for the light; and considered from this aspect, Miss Ophelia's exclamation, like Mrs. Stowe's novel, achieves a bright, almost a lurid significance, like the light from a fire which consumes a witch. . . .

Uncle Tom's Cabin is a very bad novel, having, in its self-righteous, virtuous sentimentality, much in common with *Little Women*. Sentimentality, the ostentatious parading of excessive and spurious emotion, is the mark of dishonesty, the inability to feel; the wet eyes of the sentimentalist betray his aversion to experience, his fear of life, his arid heart; and it is always, therefore, the signal of secret and violent inhumanity, the mask of cruelty; *Uncle Tom's Cabin*—like its multitudinous, hard-boiled descendants—is a catalogue of violence. This is explained by the nature of Mrs. Stowe's subject matter, her laudable determination to flinch from nothing in presenting the complete picture; an explanation which falters only if we pause to ask whether or not her picture is indeed complete; and what constriction or failure of perception forced her to so depend on the description of brutality—unmotivated, senseless—and to leave unanswered and unnoticed the only important question: what it was, after all, that moved her people to such deeds. But this, let us say, was beyond Mrs. Stowe's powers; she was not so much a novelist as an impassioned pamphleteer; her book was not intended to do anything more than prove that slavery was wrong; was, in fact, perfectly horrible. This makes material for a pamphlet but it is hardly enough for a novel; and the only question left to ask is why we are bound still within the same constriction. How is it that we are so loath to make a further journey than that made by Mrs. Stowe, to discover and reveal something a little closer to the truth? . . .

Truth, as used here, is meant to imply a devotion to the human being, his freedom and fulfillment; freedom which cannot be legislated, fulfillment which cannot be charted. This is the prime concern, the frame of reference; it is not to be confused with a devotion to Humanity which is too easily equated with a devotion to a Cause; and Causes, as we know, are notoriously bloodthirsty. . . . In overlooking, denying, evading [the complexity of the human being]—which is nothing more than the disquieting complexity of ourselves—we are diminished and we perish; only within this web of ambiguity, paradox, this hunger, danger, darkness, can we find at once ourselves and the power that will free us from ourselves. It is this power of revelation which is the business of the novelist, this journey toward a more vast reality which must take precedence over all other claims. . . . And in *Uncle Tom's Cabin* we may find . . . the formula created by the necessity to find a lie more palatable than the truth [that] has been handed down and memorized and persists yet with a terrible power.

It is interesting to consider . . . Mrs. Stowe's . . . method . . . to solve the problem of writing about a black man at all. Apart from her lively procession of field hands, house niggers, Chloe, Topsy, etc.—who are the stock, lovable figures presenting no problem—she has only three other Negroes in the book. . . . Eliza is a beautiful, pious hybrid, light enough to pass . . . differing from the genteel mistress who was overseered her education only in the respect that she is a servant. George is darker, but makes up for it by being a mechanical genius, and is, moreover, sufficiently un-Negroid to pass through town, a fugitive from his master, disguised as a Spanish gentleman, attracting no attention whatever beyond admiration. They are a race apart from Topsy. It transpires by the end of the novel, through one of those energetic, last-minute convolutions of the plot, that Eliza has some connection with French gentility. The figure from whom the novel takes its name, Uncle Tom, who is a figure of controversy yet, is jet-black, wooly-haired, illiterate; and he is phenomenally forbearing. He has to be; he is black; only through this forbearance can he survive or triumph. . . . His triumph is metaphysical, unearthly; since he is black, born without the light, it is only through humility, the incessant mortification of the flesh, that he can enter into communion with God or man. The virtuous rage of Mrs. Stowe is motivated by nothing so temporal as a concern for the relationship of men to one another—or, even, as she would have claimed, by a concern for their relationship to God—but merely by a panic of being hurled into the flames, of being caught in traffic with the devil. She embraced this merciless doctrine with all her heart, bargaining shamelessly before the throne of grace: God and salvation becoming her personal property, purchased with the coin of her virtue. Here, black equates with evil and white with grace; if, being mindful of the necessity of good works, she could not cast out the blacks—a wretched, huddled mass, apparently, claiming, like an obsession, her inner eye—she could not embrace them either without purifying them of sin. She must cover their intimidating nakedness, robe them in white, the garments of salvation; only thus could she herself be delivered from ever-present sin, only thus could she bury, as St. Paul demanded, "the carnal man, the man of the flesh." Tom, therefore, her only black man, has been robbed of his humanity and divested of his sex. It is the price for that darkness with which he has been branded.

Uncle Tom's Cabin, then, is activated by what might be called a theological terror, the terror of damnation; and the spirit that breathes in this book, hot, self-righteous, fearful, is not different from that spirit of medieval times which sought to exorcize evil by burning witches; and is not different from that terror which activates a lynch mob. One need not, indeed, search for examples so historic or so gaudy; this is a warfare waged daily in the heart, a warfare so vast, so relentless and so powerful that the interracial handshake or the interracial marriage can be as crucifying as the public hanging or the secret rape. This panic motivates our cruelty, this fear of the dark makes it impossible that our lives shall be other than superficial; this, interlocked with and feeding our glittering, mechanical, inescapable civilization which has put to death our freedom.

This, notwithstanding that the avowed aim of the American protest novel is to bring greater freedom to the oppressed. They are forgiven, on the strength of these good intentions, whatever violence they do to language, whatever excessive demands they make of credibility. It is, indeed, considered the sign of a frivolity so intense as to approach decadence to suggest that these books are both badly written and wildly improbable. One is told to put first things first, the good of society coming before the niceties of style or characterization. Even if this were incontestable—for what exactly is the "good" of society?—it argues an insuperable confusion, since literature and sociology are not one and the same; it is impossible to discuss them as if they were. Our passion for categorization, life neatly fitted into pegs, has led to an unforeseen, paradoxical distress; confusion, a breakdown of meaning. Those categories which were meant to define and control the world for us have boomeranged us into chaos; in which limbo we whirl, clutching the straws of our definitions. The "protest" novel, so far from being disturbing, is an accepted and comforting aspect of the

American scene, ramifying that framework we believe to be so necessary. Whatever unsettling questions are raised are evanescent, titillating; remote, for this has nothing to do with us, it is safely ensconced in the social arena, where, indeed, it has nothing to do with anyone, so that finally we receive a very definite thrill of virtue from the fact that we are reading such a book at all. This report from the pit reassures us of its reality and its darkness and of our own salvation; and "As long as such books are being published," an American liberal once said to me, "everything will be all right." But unless one's ideal of society is a race of neatly analyzed, hard-working ciphers, one can hardly claim for the protest novels the lofty purpose they claim for themselves or share the present optimism concerning them. They emerge for what they are: a mirror of our confusion, dishonesty, panic, trapped and immobilized in the sunlit prison of the American dream. . . .

It must be remembered that the oppressed and the oppressor are bound together within the society; they accept the same criteria, they share the same beliefs, they both alike depend on the same reality. Within this cage it is romantic, more, meaningless, to speak of a "new" society as the desire of the oppressed, for that shivering dependence on the props of reality which he shares with the Herrenvolk makes a truly "new" society impossible to conceive. . . .

Our humanity is our burden, our life; we need not battle for it; we need only to do what is infinitely more difficult—that is, accept it. The failure of the protest novel lies in its rejection of life, the human being, the denial of his beauty, dread, power, in its insistence that it is his categorization alone which is real and which cannot be transcended.

Jane P. Tompkins on Reevaluating *Uncle Tom's Cabin* and the American Literary Canon

The popular domestic novel of the nineteenth century represents a monumental effort to reorganize culture from the woman's point of view; . . . this body of work is remarkable for its intellectual complexity, ambition, and resourcefulness; and that, in certain cases, it offers a critique of American society far more devastating than any delivered by better-known critics such as Hawthorne and Melville. Finally, it suggests that the enormous popularity of these novels, which has been cause for suspicion bordering on disgust, is a reason for paying close attention to them. *Uncle Tom's Cabin* was, in almost any terms one can think of, the most important book of the century. It was the first American novel ever to sell over a million copies and its impact is generally thought to have been incalculable. Expressive of and responsible for the values of its time, it also belongs to a genre, the sentimental novel, whose chief characteristic is that it is written by, for, and about women. In this respect, *Uncle Tom's Cabin* is not exceptional but representative. It is the *summa theologica* of nineteenth-century America's religion of domesticity, a brilliant redaction of the culture's favorite story about itself—the story of salvation through motherly love. Out of the ideological materials at their disposal, the sentimental novelists elaborated a myth that gave women the central position of power and authority in the culture; and of these efforts *Uncle Tom's Cabin* is the most dazzling exemplar.

I have used words like "monumental" and "dazzling" to describe Stowe's novel and the tradition of which it is a part because they have for too long been the casualties of a set of critical attitudes that equate intellectual merit with a certain kind of argumentative discourse and certain kinds of subject matter. A long tradition of academic parochialism has enforced this sort of discourse through a series of cultural contrasts: light "feminine" novels vs. tough-minded intellectual treatises; domestic "chattiness" vs. serious thinking; and summarily, the "damned mob of scribbling women" vs. a few giant intellects, unappreciated and misunderstood in their time, struggling manfully against a flood of sentimental rubbish.[5]. . .

How deep the problem goes is illustrated dramatically by George F. Whicher's discussion of Stowe's novel in *The Literary*

History of the United States. Reflecting the consensus view on what good novels are made of, Whicher writes: "Nothing attributable to Mrs. Stowe or her handiwork can account for the novel's enormous vogue; its author's resources as a purveyor of Sunday-school fiction were not remarkable. She had at most a ready command of broadly conceived melodrama, humor, and pathos, and of these popular elements she compounded her book."[7] At a loss to understand how a book so compounded was able to "convulse a mighty nation," Whicher concludes—incredibly—that Stowe's own explanation that "God wrote it" "solved the paradox." Rather than give up his bias against "melodrama," "pathos," and "Sunday-school fiction," Whicher takes refuge in a solution that, even according to his lights, is patently absurd.[8] And no wonder. The modernist literary aesthetic cannot account for the unprecedented and persistent popularity of a book like *Uncle Tom's Cabin*, for this novel operates according to principles quite other than those that have been responsible for determining the currently sanctified American literary classics. . . .

The power of a sentimental novel to move its audience depends upon the audience's being in possession of the conceptual categories that constitute character and event. That storehouse of assumptions includes attitudes toward the family and toward social institutions; a definition of power and its relation to individual human feeling; notions of political and social equality; and above all, a set of religious beliefs that organizes and sustains the rest. Once in possession of the system of beliefs that undergirds the patterns of sentimental fiction, it is possible for modern readers to see how its tearful episodes and frequent violations of probability were invested with a structure of meanings that fixed these works, for nineteenth-century readers, not in the realm of fairy tale or escapist fantasy, but in the very bedrock of reality. I do not say that we can read sentimental fiction exactly as Stowe's audience did—that would be impossible—but that we can and should set aside the modernist prejudices which consign this fiction to oblivion, in order to see how and why it worked for its readers, in its time, with such unexampled effect.

Let us consider the episode in *Uncle Tom's Cabin* most often cited as the epitome of Victorian sentimentalism—the death of little Eva—because it is the kind of incident most offensive to the sensibilities of twentieth-century academic critics. It is on the belief that this incident is nothing more than a sob story that the whole case against sentimentalism rests. Little Eva's death, so the argument goes, like every other sentimental tale, is awash with emotion but does nothing to remedy the evils it deplores. Essentially, it leaves the slave system and the other characters unchanged. This trivializing view of the episode is grounded in assumptions about power and reality so common that we are not even aware they are in force. Thus generations of critics have commented with condescending irony on little Eva's death. But in the system of belief that undergirds Stowe's enterprise, dying is the supreme form of heroism. In *Uncle Tom's Cabin*, death is the equivalent not of defeat but of victory; it brings an access of power, not a loss of it; it is not only the crowning achievement of life, it is life, and Stowe's entire presentation of little Eva is designed to dramatize this fact.

Stories like the death of little Eva are compelling for the same reason that the story of Christ's death is compelling; they enact a philosophy, as much political as religious, in which the pure and powerless die to save the powerful and corrupt, and thereby show themselves more powerful than those they save. They enact, in short, a *theory* of power in which the ordinary or "common sense" view of what is efficacious and what is not (a view to which most modern critics are committed) is simply reversed, as the very possibility of social action is made dependent on the action taking place in individual hearts. Little Eva's death enacts the drama of which all the major episodes of the novel are transformations, the idea, central to Christian soteriology,[9] that the highest human calling is to give one's life for another. It presents one version of the ethic of sacrifice on which the entire novel is based and contains in some form all of the motifs that, by their frequent recurrence, constitute the novel's ideological framework. . . .

Of course, it could be argued by critics of sentimentalism that the prominence of stories about the deaths of children is precisely what is wrong with the literature of the period; rather than being cited as a source of strength, the presence of such stories in *Uncle Tom's Cabin* could be regarded as an unfortunate concession to the age's fondness for lachrymose scenes. But to dismiss such scenes as "all tears and flapdoodle" is to leave unexplained the popularity of the novels and sermons that are filled with them, unless we choose to believe that a generation of readers was unaccountably moved to tears by matters that are intrinsically silly and trivial. That popularity is better explained, I believe, by the relationship of these scenes to a pervasive cultural myth which invests the suffering and death of an innocent victim with just the kind of power that critics deny to Stowe's novel: the power to work in, and change, the world. . . .

If the language of tears seems maudlin and little Eva's death ineffectual, it is because both the tears and the redemption that they signify belong to a conception of the world that is now generally regarded as naive and unrealistic. Topsy's salvation and Miss Ophelia's do not alter the anti-abolitionist majority in the Senate or prevent southern plantation owners and northern investment bankers from doing business to their mutual advantage. Because most modern readers regard such political and economic facts as final, it is difficult for them to take seriously a novel that insists on religious conversion as the necessary precondition for sweeping social change. But in Stowe's understanding of what such change requires, it is the *modern* view that is naive. The political and economic measures that constitute effective action for us, she regards as superficial, mere extensions of the worldly policies that produced the slave system in the first place. Therefore, when Stowe asks the question that is in every reader's mind at the end of the novel—namely, "what can any individual do?"—she recommends not specific alterations in the current political and economic arrangements, but rather a change of heart.

Notes

5. The phrase, "a damned mob of scribbling women," coined by Hawthorne in a letter he wrote to his publisher, in 1855, and clearly

the product of Hawthorne's own feelings of frustration and envy, comes embedded in a much-quoted passage that has set the tone for criticism of sentimental fiction ever since. "America is now wholly given over to a d****d mob of scribbling women, and I should have no chance of success while the public taste is occupied with their trash—and should be ashamed of myself if I did succeed. What is the mystery of these innumerable editions of *The Lamplighter*, and other books neither better nor worse? Worse they could not be, and better they need not be, when they sell by the hundred thousand." As quoted by Fred Lewis Pattee, *The Feminine Fifties* (New York: D. Appleton-Century Co., 1940), p. 110.

7. George F. Whicher, "Literature and Conflict," in *The Literary History of the United States*, ed. Robert E. Spiller et al., 3rd ed., rev. (London: Macmillan, 1963), p. 583.

8. Whicher, in *Literary History*, ed. Spiller, p. 586. Edmund Wilson, despite his somewhat sympathetic treatment of Stowe in *Patriotic Gore: Studies in the Literature of the American Civil War* (New York: Oxford University Press, 1966), pp. 5, 32, seems to concur in this opinion, reflecting a characteristic tendency of commentators on the most popular works of sentimental fiction to regard the success of these women as some sort of mysterious eruption, inexplicable by natural causes. Henry James gives this attitude its most articulate, though perhaps least defensible, expression in a remarkable passage from *A Small Boy and Others* (New York: Charles Scribner's Sons, 1913), where he describes Stowe's book as really not a book at all but as "a fish, a wonderful 'leaping' fish"—the point being to deny Stowe any role in the process that produced such a wonder:

> Appreciation and judgment, the whole impression, were thus an effect for which there had been no process—any process so related having in other cases *had* to be at some point or other critical; nothing in the guise of a written book, therefore, a book printed, published, sold, bought and "noticed," probably ever reached its mark, the mark of exciting interest, without having at least groped for that goal *as* a book or by the exposure of some literary side. Letters, here, languished unconscious, and Uncle Tom, instead of making even one of the cheap short cuts through the medium in which books breathe, even as fishes in water, went gaily roundabout it altogether, as if a fish, a wonderful "leaping" fish, had simply flown through the air. (pp. 159–60)

9. A branch of theology that deals with salvation as the effect of divine agency [*Editor*].

Thomas F. Gossett on *Uncle Tom's Cabin* as a Measure of U.S. Race Relations

To read the opinions of *Uncle Tom's Cabin* which have been expressed over the past 130 years is something like examining a history of racism in America for this period, at least racism as it has been applied to blacks. J. C. Furnas was right when he said that *Uncle Tom's Cabin* was like a three-stage rocket—it was first powerful as a novel, then as a play, and eventually in the twentieth century as a film. It is doubtful that any work of American literature has received such a variety of interpretations, both in the reviews and criticisms it has generated and in the many ways in which it has been adapted as a play. When the novel was published in 1852, even northern reviewers in surprisingly large numbers criticized it for what they felt were exaggerated accounts of the evils of slavery. Nevertheless, it is obvious that Stowe's book was a powerful force in changing the minds of white northerners and in alerting opinion abroad to the evils of American slavery.[1]

For a long time the almost universal detestation of *Uncle Tom's Cabin* prevented all but a few readers in the South from examining it from any point of view except that of its alleged unfairness to the South and to slavery. When the Civil War was over and the white South had time to calm down, readers and critics there discovered that the novel contained ideas about blacks which might be used to suggest a more sympathetic interpretation of their own view of history. With a little judicious manipulation, many of these white southern interpreters convinced themselves that they could find in *Uncle Tom's Cabin* itself sufficient evidence to justify their own conviction that blacks ought not to have a status in society equal to that of whites. They did not wish to return to slavery, but neither did they wish to give the blacks full rights as citizens. The white South eventually came to admit, at least by implication, that slavery had been wrong, disunion had been wrong, and therefore the South's decision to initiate the Civil War had been wrong. On the other hand, they reasoned, it did not follow that the antebellum white South had been wrong in its belief in the inherent inferiority of blacks.

In the late nineteenth and early twentieth centuries, a substantial number of white northern critics of *Uncle Tom's Cabin* had also changed their opinions and had moved closer to those held by white southerners. A view frequently expressed, especially after northern disillusion with the Reconstruction of the South, was that slavery had been an evil institution and Stowe had been right to indict it. On the other hand, a surprisingly large number of white northern critics came to think Stowe had been wrong in making the black characters in her novel too noble, amiable, and intelligent to be credible. If these critics had said that her black characters generally had better qualities than people of any race, they might have had a point. Usually, however, they merely said that her black characters were presented as being better than real blacks.

In the last forty years, the current of opinion toward Stowe and *Uncle Tom's Cabin* falls chiefly into three categories. Black critics and scholars strongly reject the novel, deploring the frequent recourse to racist explanations of the traits of the characters, especially those of the blacks. A great many white critics—probably a majority—also reject the novel but principally because they find it almost wholly lacking in literary merit. There is a third group, however, who have something like the enthusiasm of earlier critics for both the author and her book. Nearly all of these critics are white, and to those who reject the novel on literary grounds, these critics say that Stowe's faults are a matter of style rather than of substance. They argue that while she used the form of the sentimental and domestic novel, she was able to transcend that form because she had a broad grasp of human nature and was able to analyze both institutions and individual characters with great insight. To the black critics who deplore the novel, the white critics who admire it generally concede that it contains serious faults in its interpretation of the black characters. They argue, however, that Stowe's racism belongs to her time and place. They see her as struggling, and with considerable success, to free herself from it. Properly understood, they argue, the racism is not sufficient to invalidate the novel, and they conclude that Stowe was able not merely to analyze slavery perceptively but to present credible characters, black and white, reacting to a monstrous institution.

Note

1. Furnas, *Goodbye to Uncle Tom*, p. 254.

ROBERT S. LEVINE ON STOWE AND FREDERICK DOUGLASS

In a much discussed moment near the end of *Uncle Tom's Cabin*, the light-skinned "black" George Harris, after having spent nine years away from the United States, chooses to embrace what he terms "an African *nationality*." He maintains that those of "the African race" have "peculiarities"—domestic attachments, lack of social competitiveness—that promise to bring forth in Liberia an "essentially . . . Christian" nation far superior to the nominally Christian United States. For this to occur, he claims, that nation must have "a tangible, separate existence of its own" on "the shores of Africa." Harris thus links race to place in ways similar to the Liberian colonizationists, who sought to remove blacks from the United States, even as he distances himself from the racism of the American Colonization Society by theorizing that God's providential hand lies behind Liberia's founding. But the fact that many of the novel's former slaves end up going to Africa suggests that Stowe uses George Harris as a mouthpiece to forward her own colonizationist views that blacks belong in Africa, whites in America.[1]

Yet Harris makes his back-to-Africa argument in the larger context of a social critique of the failure of the United States to live up to its political ideals and moral obligations, particularly given the crucial role African Americans have played in the development of the nation. He declares: "We *ought* to be free . . . to rise by our individual worth, without any consideration of caste or color; and they who deny us this right are false to their own professed principles of human equality. We ought, in particular, to be allowed *here*." Harris's rhetoric is similar to that used by Douglass and Delany in the *North Star*, and it is of a piece with the rhetoric Douglass would continue to use during the 1850s to challenge colonizationists and emigrationists alike. Stowe herself, in a rarely commented-upon moment in the closing pages of the novel, would also seem to have distanced herself from George Harris's African nationalism when she lists, "on the authority of Professor C. E. Stowe," a number of former slaves who have gone on to live economically successful lives in the United States. These enterprising African Americans, she declares, testify to "the self-denial, energy, patience, and honesty, which the slave has exhibited in a state of freedom." Rather than using her examples to support colonizationism, she enlists them to show that blacks have the capacity, particularly when treated in Christian fashion, to rise in the United States to "highly respectable stations in society. . . . Douglas [*sic*] and [Samuel] Ward among editors, are well known instances." By adducing on the last page of the novel the example of Douglass in particular, Stowe, it is worth underscoring, links herself with the African American who, for the past decade or so, had most passionately contested the notion that blacks "belong" in Africa.[2]

This brief discussion of race and nation in *Uncle Tom's Cabin* suggests that the novel remains conflicted on these interrelated issues. On the one hand, Stowe develops providential and racialist arguments for encouraging U.S. blacks to "return" to Africa; on the other hand, she proffers moral-reform ideology to suggest that blacks can and should prosper in the United States. Given the novel's own conflicted allegiances, it is not surprising that the response of literate free blacks of the North was equally conflicted. Outraged and despairing over the Fugitive Slave Law, a number of blacks, most notably Frederick Douglass, regarded *Uncle Tom's Cabin*, as Richard Yarborough puts it, "as a godsend destined to mobilize white sentiment against slavery just when resistance to the southern forces was urgently needed." Many other blacks, however, most notably Martin Delany, were resentful that such massive cultural authority was bestowed on a white woman who, so they argued, was at heart a racist colonizationist.[3] But ironically, even as Delany attacked Stowe's colonizationism, he set forth the racialized view that blacks should consider leaving the United States through a program of voluntary emigration. For Douglass, who endorsed Stowe's moral reformism, Delany's criticisms of Stowe and his development of an emigrationist politics were shortsighted and contradictory; for Delany, Douglass's embrace of a novel (and a nation) that ultimately wanted to rid itself of blacks revealed the fatal consequences of a politics of accommodation.

In short, some of the key debates of the early to mid-1850s on race and nation were spawned by the African American response to *Uncle Tom's Cabin*. . . . Douglass, who viewed the black "nation" within the United States as the result of whites' racial prejudices, persisted in underscoring the importance of black newspapers, conventions, and self-help as pragmatic means toward improving the situation of African Americans. In contrast, by 1852 Delany sought to empower that black "nation" by locating it outside the boundaries of the United States. In his advocacy of black emigration, which he presented, as opposed to colonizationism, as black-led and a matter of free choice, Delany pushed the debate on blacks' condition in the United States beyond the stark binarism of Liberian colonizationism versus black elevation by imagining for African Americans possibilities in a third place that was within the Americas but not a part of the United States—Central and South America and the Caribbean.

My focus in this chapter, a study of the intersection of literary reception and cultural (re)action, will be on the ways in which Delany's and Douglass's conflicting responses to Stowe's novel came to inform their writings and politics of the 1852–55 period. Douglass and Delany debated Stowe's novel partly because they had a principled disagreement over its politics and partly because each wanted to be the main voice for the black community. Their differences fed on themselves on intertwining personal and political levels, serving to drive the former coeditors further apart and into opposing camps. Douglass continued to lay claim to black leadership through his representative status as the embodiment of African Americans' possibilities in the United States. Delany, over the course of his early 1850s debates with Douglass, increasingly came to lay his own claim to black leadership through a very different sort of representative identity: as the mystical and biological embodiment of black possibility in the Americas. . . .

In *Key*, Stowe adduced Douglass's *Narrative* as a source that corroborated (and inspired) her depiction of George Harris's ability to sustain his "intelligent and active mind through all the squalid misery, degradation, and oppression of slavery." But in the midst of writing *Uncle Tom's Cabin* Stowe wanted more from Douglass than the published record of his 1845 autobiography, and on 9 July 1851 (to consider from a different perspective some of the material discussed in Chapter 2), she wrote him asking for information on the workings of cotton plantations. She explains herself as follows: "I have before me an able paper written by a Southern planter, in which the details and *modus operandi* are given from his point of sight. I am anxious to have something from another standpoint." That additional "standpoint," she suggests, will help make her picture of the cotton plantation "true to nature in its details." Clearly, for Stowe a central "detail" of any representation of southern plantations is an "authenticating" black perspective. Her desire to incorporate into her work blacks' "point of sight" is evident not only in her inquiry to Douglass but also in her revelation in the same letter that she has become a subscriber to his paper and has "read it with great interest." It is precisely her reading of Douglass's paper that has raised questions in her mind about his positions on two large issues—"the church and African colonization"—and as part of an effort to establish a dialogue with Douglass, she states her desire to change his views. She does so, however, with a full recognition that she addresses an intelligent individual who may well resist her ideas: "I would willingly, if I could, modify your views on both points." Although she has nothing specific to say about colonization, she does defend the antislavery work of her father, Lyman Beecher (a colonizationist), and of other ministers in her family, maintaining that the church has "the purest and most high-principled men and women of the country."[10]

Though Stowe, through George Harris, endorses Liberian colonization in *Uncle Tom's Cabin*, it is a tentative endorsement at best, for she uses George Harris's rationalizing remarks on God's deeper spiritual purpose in establishing the colony to expose the racism that underlies whites' commitment to the movement. And though critical of the pro-slavery ministers praised by Marie St. Clare, she reserves her greatest scorn for the hypocritical ministers of Northern churches who remain in silent complicity with proslavery practices. If Stowe in her 1851 letter set out to "correct" Douglass, the rhetoric of her novel suggests that Douglass, through the columns of his newspaper, "corrected" Stowe instead.

Notes

1. Harriet Beecher Stowe, *Uncle Tom's Cabin; or, Life among the Lowly*, ed. Elizabeth Ammons (New York: W. W. Norton, 1994), pp. 374, 375. Founded in 1816, the American Colonization Society (ACS) sought to encourage free blacks to emigrate to the colony of Liberia. Central to the society's beliefs was the notion that whites and blacks could not live together in the United States. Stowe's father, Lyman Beecher, was a prominent supporter of the ACS.

2. Stowe, *Uncle Tom's Cabin*, pp. 375, 386, 387, 388. For a different reading of the novel's cataloguing of free blacks in the final pages, see Gillian Brown, *Domestic Individualism: Imagining Self in Nineteenth-Century America* (Berkeley: University of California Press, 1990), pp. 58–59.

3. Richard Yarborough, "Strategies of Black Characterization in *Uncle Tom's Cabin* and the Early Afro-American Novel," in *New Essays on "Uncle Tom's Cabin,"* ed. Eric J. Sundquist (New York: Cambridge University Press, 1986), p. 68. For a useful overview of African American debate on *Uncle Tom's Cabin*, see Marva Banks, "Uncle Tom's Cabin and Antebellum Black Response," in *Readers in History: Nineteenth-Century American Literature and the Contexts of Response*, ed. James L. Machor (Baltimore: Johns Hopkins University Press, 1993), pp. 209–27. Banks overstates blacks' resistance to the novel, arguing that the majority of blacks at mid-century regarded *Uncle Tom's Cabin* as "a curse that encouraged continuation of

the doctrine of white supremacy in America" (225). The positive response of Douglass and his many associates to Stowe's novel belies this generalization; see, for example, the discussion below of the 1853 Rochester convention. On the response of modern African American critics to *Uncle Tom's Cabin*, see Thomas F. Gossett, "Uncle Tom's Cabin and American Culture" (Dallas: Southern Methodist University Press, 1985), pp. 388–96. Surely the most influential attack on the novel by an African American writer has been James Baldwin's "Everybody's Protest Novel" (1949), which excoriates Stowe for her "self-righteous, virtuous sentimentality" (rpt. in *Critical Essays on Harriet Beecher Stowe*, ed. Elizabeth Ammons [Boston: G. K. Hall, 1980], p. 92).

10. Stowe, *Key*, p. 16 (see also pp. 17–18); Stowe to Douglass, letter of 9 July 1859, in *Life and Letters of Harriet Beecher Stowe*, ed. Annie Fields (Boston: Houghton, Mifflin, 1897), pp. 133–34. William S. McFeely notes that Stowe was on the subscription list of Douglass's *North Star* (*Frederick Douglass* [New York: W. W. Norton, 1991], p. 152).

Elizabeth Ammons on Stowe's Endorsement of the "Liberian Solution"

Conceived by Southern planters, unsupported by most African Americans, opposed by abolitionists, and rapidly and repeatedly resisted by Africans, Liberia was always a contested idea. How, then, does one read the endorsement of colonization in *Uncle Tom's Cabin*?

Stowe places her support for Liberian emigration in the mouth of George Harris (374–76), her smartest, whitest, most militant black—which, of course, goes a long way toward explaining her endorsement of an idea that abolitionists from Douglass to Garrison roundly condemned. Deportation conveniently solves the problem of dealing with demands for racial equality in America. If at the end of *Uncle Tom's Cabin* George Harris remained in the United States, or even just across the border in Canada, how would Stowe contain his militant voice not just for emancipation but also for black equality? Imagine Tom living rather than dying, and the point becomes obvious. Tom would never be a problem because he would always be a servant. George Harris, however, does present difficulties. Educated, enraged, determined not to acquiesce in American racism, he represents a character potentially out of the author's control: an articulate advocate for racial equality in the United States. Similarly, Topsy, "civilized" and educated, represents a threat, as do an independent Eliza, the Harris children, Cassy, and, quickly mentioned at the very end, Cassy's son, an educated "young man of energy" (377). Consequently Stowe, in the tested tradition of the ACS, packs them all off to Africa, the place for dangerous, ambitious, free American blacks.

Yet if Stowe's endorsement of emigration reflects her racism, and it does, it also and paradoxically signifies her respect for African Americans' full equality as fellow Christians, world, missionaries, and, therefore, potentially glorious imperialists. Even those opposed to Liberian colonization in the nineteenth century did not oppose it because it was wrong to inflict Western religion, social codes, and economic systems on people who already had their own cultural practices and beliefs. For blacks and whites alike, imperialism was not the issue; exiling African Americans was. Therefore we need to ask: is it possible to think of Stowe's endorsement of Liberian colonization both as a racist plot to deport American blacks and as an idealistic imperialist project (hard as it is for us to put those terms together), with black people rather than whites in the lead? The opposition of leaders such as Douglass and Garrison, the history of Liberia, and progressive condemnation of imperialism today make it difficult to find anything positive in Stowe's support for African American colonization of Liberia. Nevertheless, we need to note that Stowe assigns to black Americans the same respected nineteenth-century status enjoyed or aspired to by many white Americans, that of pioneer or settler, which is to say, imperialist. She includes African Americans as primary actors in the nineteenth-century western drama of colonizing the globe in the name of Christianity and Western civilization. To remind ourselves that, like Stowe, many of our predecessors viewed colonialism positively, or at the very least uncritically, consider the respected African American historian Benjamin Brawley's description of Liberian settlers:

> If we compare them with the Pilgrim Fathers, we find that as the Pilgrims had to subdue the Indians, so they had to hold their own against a score of aggressive tribes. The Pilgrims had the advantage of a thousand years of culture and experience in government; the Negroes, only recently out of bondage, had been deprived of any opportunity for improvement whatsoever. (191)

That Americans might take pride in not living up to the Pilgrim Fathers' brutal example reflects my, not Brawley's, view.

In the final analysis, however, there is no rationalizing the racism of Stowe's Liberian solution, which readers have rightly criticized from the beginning (see, e.g., Allen). Reacting to attacks, Stowe herself in a letter to the American and Foreign Anti-Slavery Society regretted sending George Harris to Africa (R. Levine 536); and, clearly, even as she wrote *Uncle Tom's Cabin*, she knew her position required strenuous defense. She has George Harris try to rebut the standard anti-colonization arguments of her day. He concedes that "the scheme may have been used, in unjustifiable ways, as a means of retarding our emancipation" and acknowledges that emigrants could be seen as turning their backs on fellow African Americans. In response, he maintains that a sovereign black nation in Africa would have power to speak "in the council of nations" worldwide: "A nation has a right to argue, remonstrate, implore, and present the cause of its race,—which an individual has not" (375). Most important, his motive for leaving the United States is the same as that of Liberian immigrants I have quoted. George renounces the United States—"I have no wish to pass for an American, or to identify myself with them" (374)—and, Afrocentrically, chooses Africa as his home. While the rhetoric is Victorian, the sentiment anticipates Marcus Garvey and W. E. B. Du Bois. George says, "I go to *my country*,—my chosen, my glorious Africa!" (376).

But then Stowe tips her hand entirely. Immediately following George's proud, impassioned denunciation of United States racism, she dispatches every educated black American in her book to Africa (377). George's rhetoric simply establishes the pretext for removing all powerful black opponents of racism in *Uncle Tom's Cabin*. Completing the picture, she next shows us the uneducated, newly freed blacks on the Shelby plantation so grateful to their magnanimous young white master that they vow never to leave the plantation (379). Stowe wants slavery to end and racial inequality to remain. There is no other conclusion.

Marianne Noble on Stowe's Sentimentalism

Stowe had contempt for dishonest forms of sentimentality. . . . She also recognized, however, that the epithet "sentimental" was all too frequently slapped dismissively onto any discourse that valued feelings. In *Uncle Tom's Cabin*, for example, Senator Bird ridicules "all sentimental weakness of those who would put the welfare of a few miserable fugitives before great state interests" (155). Likewise, St. Clare recalls that his brother had accused him of "a womanish sentimentalism" for sympathizing with slaves (342). . . . Female authors turned to high sentimentality in order to redress the cognitive failures of abstract analysis that they believed had led the nation into its great moral crisis. They believed that detached abstraction served as the basis of the corrupt legal system. As Mrs. Bird puts it, "I hate reasoning . . . on such subjects. There's a way you political folks have of coming round and round a plain right thing; and you don't believe in it yourselves when it comes to practice" (145). She advocates a sentimental alternative: "Your heart is better than your head, in this case" (153).[3]

In pursuing her sentimental epistemology, Stowe relied upon a conviction that nonslaves could know what the pain of slavery felt like. When her son Charley died, she identified her emotional anguish with that felt by slave parents whose children were sold to other masters. "It was at his dying bed and at his grave that I learned what a poor slave mother may feel when her child is torn away from her," she wrote.[4] Like many sentimental authors, Stowe saw the anguish of bereavement as a universal emotion that cut through cultural difference, enabling one person to understand perfectly what another was feeling. In *Uncle Tom's Cabin*, for instance, when Tom is torn from his wife and children, Stowe emphasizes the universality of his grief: "Sobs, heavy, hoarse, and loud, shook the chair, and great tears fell through his fingers on the floor; just such tears, sir, as you dropped into the coffin where lay your first born son; such tears, woman, as you shed when you heard the cries of your dying babe. For, sir, he was a man,—and you are but another man. And, woman, though dressed in silk and jewels, you are but a woman, and, in life's great straits and mighty grief, ye feel but one sorrow!" (90–91). The anguish of separation is a unifying force, for all races, classes, and genders experience bereavement as "one sorrow." Here we see the classic paradox of sentimentalism, which is that the pain of separation fosters a unity of feeling among sufferers.

In *Uncle Tom's Cabin* Stowe capitalizes upon the political potential of this paradox of sentimental separation. In order to forge between readers and slaves a union based upon shared feelings, she reinvigorates readers' own anguished memories of bereavement and separation, suggesting that those experiences are qualitatively the same as the miseries of slavery.[5] . . . The senator's approach epitomizes prevailing epistemologies; he supports the Fugitive Slave Law because he thinks in dehumanizing abstractions, such as "fugitives," and never considers the emotions of the human beings represented by these abstractions: "his idea of a fugitive was only an idea of the letters that spell the word,—or at the most, the image of a little newspaper picture of a man with a stick and bundle with "Ran away from the subscriber" under it. The magic of the real presence of distress,—the imploring human eye, the frail, trembling human hand, the despairing appeal of helpless agony,—these he had never tried" (156). He is reformed by a sentimental wound. When Eliza Harris attempts to explain why she ran away from the Shelbys, she interrupts the senator's series of logical questions with a question of her own that shifts the epistemological basis of the discussion. She asks if the Birds have ever lost a child, a question that was "thrust on a new wound." When the Birds answer yes, Eliza explains, "Then you will feel for me. I have lost two" (148). This fictional example illustrates Stowe's own literary method: she thrusts into readers' preexisting wounds, forcing them to "feel for" slaves by reexperiencing their own painful separations and other forms of suffering. This wounding forces a new mode of cognition upon readers, who are to understand slavery through their memories of sorrow rather than through reason, and thereby apprehend the "plain right thing" that logic conceals.[6]

Notes

3. Even an ambitious, feminist author such as Margaret Fuller can be called sentimental. In *Woman in the Nineteenth Century*, Fuller promotes a recognizably "high sentimental" epistemology, calling for a greater fluidity between genders that would restore to men their repressed, female "intuitive" and "electrical" qualities. High sentimentality is an epistemology devoted to emotive and kinetic cognition. It can produce rigorous writing or "rancid writing," as Ann Douglas puts it, depending upon the talent of its user. Douglas, however, is quite right to observe that sentimentality frequently fails to meet the high literary goals of its theorizers. Camfield offers a useful hypothesis that high sentimentality degenerated as its practitioners lost sight of the genre's roots in Common Sense philosophy. See Sandra Gustafson for a discussion of Fuller's sentimentality.

4. C. E. Stowe, 203–4.

5. See Nudelman's analysis of the sentimental authors' ideal of a community of free and enslaved women bonded through suffering.

6. This presumption that sympathy will reveal the "plain right thing" characterizes Martha Nussbaum's recent appeal on behalf of the literary imagination in public discourse, *Poetic Justice*. Grounding her argument in Smith's *Theory of Moral Sentiments* which she unequivocally endorses, Nussbaum argues that contemporary judges and economists would benefit from the "put-yourself-in-his-shoes" kind of reasoning that Smith and Stowe idealize; they would then be more likely to perceive the right course of action, which purely rational arguments are less liable to reveal. I address the political limitations of sympathy more fully at the end of this chapter.

Samuel Otter on the Race Question: Uncle Tom, Topsy, and Miss Ophelia

Much of the critical attention to questions of race in *Uncle Tom's Cabin* has focused on the prominent figure of Tom.[5] According to Stowe, he "was a large, broad-chested, powerfully-made man, of a full glossy black, and a face whose truly African features were characterized by an expression of grave and steady good sense, united with much kindliness and benevolence."[6] With "the soft, impressible nature of his kindly race, ever yearning toward the simple and the childlike" (127), he is drawn to the young Eva St. Clare, the daughter of his Louisiana master. Like his fellow Africans, he receives the Gospel "with eager docility" (343). . . .

The slavetrader Haley seems to get it right when he markets Tom to Augustine St. Clare as "all the moral and Christian virtues bound in black morocco" (129). Tom is less a person than a glossy package, a beautifully bound and stereotyped book of virtues. He is bound in various senses: legally, by slavery; racially, by his skin; theologically, by his Christian destiny; and ideologically, by Stowe. . . . Most of the characters in *Uncle Tom's Cabin*, black and white, are not intended to be the realistic portrayals whose absence is lamented by many critics. They are the products of Stowe's uncanny ability in her first novel to give eloquent form to ideas about character and to discern and recast types: the little blonde evangelist, the anguished quadroon, the discontented mulatto, the sensitive (and ultimately ineffective) master, the selfish mistress, the vicious master (from New England), the conscientious spinster (who becomes conscious of her prejudice), and the Christian slave (the darker, the more devout). Stowe makes her arguments through these types. . . .

Is the portrait of Tom racist? Racialist? Progressive? Repellent? Heartbreaking? Has Tom been emasculated? Feminized? If feminized, for good or for ill? Part of the answer has to do with what the historian George Frederickson has called Stowe's northern "romantic racialism," her view in *Uncle*

Tom's Cabin that racial differences were essential and permanent but not hierarchical.[7] . . .

"Romantic" racialism, I suppose, is preferable to "classical" racism, especially in the context of the vehement racial politics of the 1850s. Stowe's efforts to elevate her African-American characters to leading roles in the next, more truly Christian phase of history should not be dismissed, given the Negrophobia she sought to counter. These advances come with a cost, though. . . .

In the character of Miss Ophelia, the most psychologically interesting portrayal in *Uncle Tom's Cabin*, Stowe dramatizes the challenge of identification and reveals her own difficulty in imagining the aftermath of slavery. Ophelia's depth may be due partly to the ways in which she reflects and rearranges her author's character. Like Stowe, Ophelia is a product of New England Calvinism. . . . Like Stowe, Ophelia is conscientious, conscience being "the granite formation" of New England women, according to the narrator (138). Ophelia "thought with great strength within certain narrow limits" (137). She is energetic: "It really was a labor to see her" working, the narrator observes (206). Unlike Stowe, who, according to her husband Calvin, lacked the skills of domestic management, Ophelia is "a living impersonation of order, method, and exactness" (137). Her life is literally compartmentalized: "There she is, sitting now in her state-room, surrounded by a mixed multitude of little and big carpetbags, boxes, baskets, each containing some separate responsibility which she is tying, binding up, packing, or fastening, with a face of great earnestness" (138). The exaggerations of Ophelia's character often come with a knowing irony. Ophelia is eager for custodianship: her "keen, dark eyes had a peculiarly searching, advised movement, and travelled over everything, as if they were looking for something to take care of" (137). The impressive thing about Ophelia, though, is that her region and her religion define her limits but also press her to exceed them. An "absolute bond-slave of the '*ought*'" (138), she is burdened with a scrupulousness and zeal that haunt her with a sense of deficiency and goad her to improve.

The most difficult limit Ophelia encounters is her racial discomfort, the "sin" of New England "prejudice of caste and color," as Stowe describes it in her analysis of Ophelia in *A Key to Uncle Tom's Cabin.*[11] Stowe incarnates this problem in Topsy, whom her cousin Augustine St. Clare has purchased for her partly as an intellectual joke. Topsy is meant as a test of Ophelia's New England pieties about the duty of educating African Americans under slavery. Ophelia flinches not only at the task but also at the presence of the "heathenish" girl (207). Earlier, arriving at her cousin's New Orleans mansion, Ophelia had been repelled by the sight of Eva kissing Mammy and sitting on Tom's knee. After the Tom incident, St. Clare comments on the distance between the abstract affection of northerners and their personal revulsion for enslaved African Americans. His barbs come with many edges: "You would not have them abused; but you don't want anything to do with them yourselves. You would send them to Africa out of your sight and smell, and then send a missionary or two to do up all the self-denial of elevating them compendiously" (154). Thoughtful, as always, Ophelia admits that her cousin may be right. In a small but telling echo (and critics often miss the small moments in this grandiose book), St. Clare uses words with Ophelia—"You loathe them as you would a snake or a toad" (154)—that Topsy later repeats to Eva. After the little evangelist assures Topsy that Ophelia would love her if Topsy were good, she responds: "No; she can't bar me, 'cause I'm a nigger!—she'd soon have a toad touch her!" (245) It is as though Topsy had overheard St. Clare and Ophelia treating her as a specimen.

Topsy is black, ragged, and tricky. She is less a character than an anarchic force, an anti-Ophelia. Her antics (or they may be tactics) constitute some of the more embarrassing moments in the novel. In *A Key to Uncle Tom's Cabin*, sensing that there was something inadequate about her rendering of Topsy, Stowe provides social background and psychological analysis. She offers retrospective directions for reading. Topsy is the emblematic product of racism, southern and northern. Degraded by a sense of imposed inferiority, "urged on by a kind of secret desperation," she uses her ingenuity to confirm her status (*Key*, 91).

Miss Ophelia recoils from Topsy, but she is also drawn to her. She is drawn from a sense of duty, but also from something more than duty. . . . In *Uncle Tom's Cabin*, Stowe represents Ophelia as being altered by Topsy's grief after Eva's death. Ophelia assures Topsy that she is capable of loving her, "having learned something of the love of Christ" from Eva. The narrator tells us that Ophelia's voice and her "honest tears" communicated more than her words and that, for the first time, she has an influence over the girl (259).

At the end of *Uncle Tom's Cabin*, we are briefly informed that Ophelia has brought Topsy back to Vermont to live in her house, despite the resistance of the locals, and that she has educated and disciplined her. Baptized and a church member, Topsy is now a missionary in Africa. The limits of Stowe's imagination in *Uncle Tom's Cabin* are vivid here. She can only gesture toward a freedom for Topsy, and this freedom involves her submission and removal. . . .

Ophelia is at the center of the book. The two chapters that bridge the end of the first and the beginning of the second volume, Chapters XVIII and XIX, are both titled "Miss Ophelia's Experiences and Opinions." In these chapters, Ophelia unsuccessfully tries to systematize Dinah's kitchen and she discusses the condition and future of the United States with her cousin. St. Clare argues that the exploitation of human beings corrupts south and north, the United States and England, and he suggests, partly out of conviction and partly out of ennui, that a day of wrath is at hand in which the masses of the world will rise up against their masters. Balanced against this prophecy is the alternative of what both St. Clare and Ophelia refer to as social "experiment" (203, 215). St. Clare describes how he subdued a defiant slave named Scipio through kindness (a story which sends Eva into a fit of weeping), and Ophelia, in Chapter XX, begins her test of character with Topsy. St. Clare's experiment is one-sided and paternalistic; Ophelia's experiment opens up and then closes down. Stowe will rethink her ideas about revolution and experiment in her next anti-slavery novel, the aptly titled *Dred*.

Notes

5. Significant essays on Stowe and race include those found in Eric J. Sundquist's collection *New Essays on Uncle Tom's Cabin* (New York: Cambridge University Press, 1986), especially Sundquist's "Introduction," 1–44, Richard Yarborough, "Strategies of black characterization in *Uncle Tom's Cabin* and the early Afro-American novel," 45–84, and Elizabeth Ammons, "Stowe's dream of the mother-savior: *Uncle Tom's Cabin* and American women writers before the 1920s," 155–95 Hortense J. Spillers, "Changing the letter: the yokes, the jokes of discourse; or, Mrs. Stowe, Mr. Reed," in Deborah E. McDowell and Arnold Rampersad, eds., *Slavery and the Literary Imagination* (Baltimore: Johns Hopkins University Press, 1989), 25–61; Christina Zwarg, "Fathering and blackface in *Uncle Tom's Cabin*," *Novel: A Forum on Fiction* 22.3 (Spring 1989), 274–87; Arthur Riss, "Racial essentialism and family values in *Uncle Tom's Cabin*," *American Quarterly* 46.4 (Dec. 1994), 513–44; and Michael J. Meyer, "Toward a rhetoric of equality: reflective and refractive images in Stowe's language," in *The Stowe Debate: Rhetorical Strategies in Uncle Tom's Cabin*, ed. Mason I. Lowance, Jr., Ellen E. Westbrook, and R. C. De Prospo (Amherst: University of Massachusetts Press, 1994) 236–54. For books, see the Stowe chapters in Jane P. Tompkins, *Sensational Designs: The Cultural Work of American fiction, 1790–1860* (New York: Oxford University Press, 1985); Philip Fisher, *Hard Facts: Setting and Form in the American Novel* (Cambridge: Harvard University Press, 1985); Gillian Brown, *Domestic Individualism: Imagining Self in Nineteenth-Century America* (Berkeley: University of California Press, 1990); Lora Romero, *Home Fronts: Domesticity and its Critics in the Antebellum United States* (Durham: Duke University Press, 1997); and Gregg D. Crane, *Race, Citizenship, and Law in American Literature* (New York: Cambridge University Press, 2002). See also Joan D. Hedrick, *Harriet Beecher Stowe: A Life* (New York: Oxford University Press, 1994).

6. Harriet Beecher Stowe, *Uncle Tom's Cabin*, ed. Elizabeth Ammons (W. W. Norton & Co., Inc., 1994) 18.

7. On "romantic racialism," see George M. Frederickson, *The Black Image in the White Mind* (New York: Harper Collins, 1971), 97–129 Mia Bay analyzes the African-American version, in which "messianic ethnologists" imagined that theirs was the "redeemer race." See *The White Image in the Black Mind: African-American Ideas about White People, 1830–1925* (New York: Oxford University Press, 2000), 38–74.

11. Harriet Beecher Stowe, *A Key to Uncle Tom's Cabin* (rpt. New York: Arno Press and the New York Times, 1969), 51–52.

Cindy Weinstein on Stowe's Response to the Southern Response

When Stowe urged her readers to "feel right," she assumed that a position against slavery had to follow. She was wrong, according to many southerners, who "looked to their sympathies in these matters" and were convinced that slavery expressed their sympathy for African Americans. Many argued that masters, not slaves, deserved sympathy given the burdens of caring for slaves who had been inherited, like it or not, and the unfair assault that Stowe had launched against southern character. Louisa J. McCord's 1853 review of *Uncle Tom's Cabin* begins with this tableau of self-pity: "Truly it would seem that the labour of Sisyphus is laid upon us, the slaveholders of these southern United States." Mary Eastman's *Aunt Phillis's Cabin* denounces Stowe, "In what an attitude, O Planters of the South, has Mrs. Stowe taken your likenesses!" And Caroline Rush's *The North and South, or, Slavery and its Contrasts: A Tale of Real Life* begins with an extended reply to Stowe in which Rush claims, "I would never refuse to do a kind action for a person because that person happened to be black, but I would far rather relieve the suffering of my own colour, because I believe they stand far more in need of relief, and are far less apt to be relieved."[12] In arguing against Stowe, defenders of slavery adopted various strategies. They maintained the greater suffering of whites over blacks in order to redirect the circuits of sympathy toward masters, toward northern white workers, toward the British factory workers, toward anyone *but* slaves. They also argued that one of the master's primary duties, in contrast to the purely economic function of factory owners, was the proper dispensation of sympathy toward his slaves.

Sympathy was a key term in the antebellum lexicon, as literary critics and historians have shown, and the debate about *Uncle Tom's Cabin* (as well as the novel itself) underscores this point. Not only does the word appear throughout the novel, but the act of extending or withholding sympathy functions as one of the most reliable indicators of a person's character.

Sympathy is one of the hallmarks of the narrator's style (she writes, "we forbear, out of sympathy to our readers" [78]), as well as one of the defining features, according to Stowe, of "the negro [who is] sympathetic" (291). In contrast to the "real sympathy" (84) that is registered when Aunt Chloe and Mrs. Shelby mourn Tom's departure, Maria responds to Prue's relentless tale of suffering, "I don't feel a particle of sympathy for such cases" (202). Eva's response to Prue's story—"these things *sink into my heart*" (204)—stands as a counter-image to Maria's callousness.

Stowe's attack on slavery was so effective, so blistering because she argued that slavery was only possible in the absence of sympathy. She had not just misrepresented the south, but, worse, she had impugned the region's sympathies, its collective heart. From Stowe's perspective, the precondition of slavery was the legalized refusal to acknowledge that slaves had feelings and the legalized inability of (potentially sympathetic) masters to do anything about it, whether teaching them how to read, allowing them to marry, or freeing them. Defenders of slavery, therefore, found themselves not only defending their facts but their feelings. That southerners had feelings at all was something that many felt required proof, especially when advertisements for the novel included pronouncements such as "he who can read this greatest of all American Tales unmoved, must have been very successful in hardening his heart," or "these volumes will be read South as well as North, and find response in every honest heart." . . .

A Key records Stowe's own rereading of *Uncle Tom's Cabin* in the context of southern responses, and it is a devastating counter-attack. . . . Its opening chapter characterizes *Uncle Tom's Cabin* as an "arrangement of real incidents—of actions really performed, of words and expressions really uttered" (5). By way of contrast, Stowe quotes J. Thornton Randolph's *The Cabin and Parlor*, which maintains that slave families are separated in "*novels*," but not "in real life, except in rare cases." She then asks the question that had been asked of her book, "Are these representations true?" (133). Stowe's answer is a resounding no, and her critique proceeds by reproducing advertisements for

"NEGROES WANTED" (139) and "NEGROES FOR SALE" (135) Stowe's rage at such mendacity is evident, and expressions of southern benevolence are juxtaposed with advertisements describing slaves with missing teeth or toes. She intersperses searing readings of the perfidious language of "indefinite terms" (142) used to describe slaves for sale, such as "*selected*" (142) "assortment" (142) and "lots" (142), all of which help Stowe prove that *Uncle Tom's Cabin* is true and *The Cabin and Parlor* is false. . . .

Southern responses to *Uncle Tom's Cabin* demanded that Stowe recuperate sympathy for the anti-slavery cause, which she does in *A Key*. . . . Stowe's rereading of her novel in light of pro-slavery appropriations of her call to "feel right" provides us with an important model for reevaluating our understanding of sympathy to include kinds of affect and modes of expression not usually associated with sympathy, such as irony, citation, and facts.

Note

12. Louisa J. McCord, "Uncle Tom's Cabin," in *Southern Quarterly Review* 23 (January 1853), 82; Mrs. Mary E. Eastman, *Aunt Phillis's Cabin; or, Southern Life as It Is* (Philadelphia: Lippincott, Grambo & Co. 1852), 268; Caroline E. Rush, *The North and South, or, Slavery and its Contrasts: A Tale of Real Life* (Philadelphia: Crissy and Markley, 1852), 14.

Joy Jordan-Lake on Stowe's Elevation of Women

Stowe's work [concurs] with . . . others of the domestic novelists, on presenting women as primarily hearth and family-centered creatures—yet Stowe deftly transforms this role from a limitation to a source of empowerment. As Elizabeth Ammons has said: "Harriet Beecher Stowe displays in *Uncle Tom's Cabin* a facility for converting essentially repressive concepts of femininity into a positive (and activist) alternative system of values in which woman figures not merely as the moral superior of man, his inspirer, but as the model for him in the new millennium about to dawn" ("Heroines" 163). While Stowe's agreeing that home was "the appointed sphere for woman" classifies her as traditionalist by twenty-first-century standards, she grants women ecclesiastical authority that extends beyond the sweet, diminutive, passive household angel. . . . In contrast to proslavery sentimentalists, the female characters of *Uncle Tom's Cabin* do not hesitate to defy husbands, fathers, and slave masters when their own ethics clash with socially prescribed submission, and are presented as or in some cases evolve into mother-saviors: Eliza physically saves her child through superhuman feats and saves her husband's soul through what Stowe presents as the young woman's steadfast faith; Rachel Halliday assists in redeeming fugitive slaves, even as she serves as her Quaker community's center of comfort and instruction; Mrs. Bird opposes her husband's domestic authority and federal law in harboring fugitives; Mrs. Shelby and Chloe conspire to protect Eliza; and the child Eva, whose name derives from the biblical Eve, which in Hebrew means "mother of all living," comforts and catechizes her father's slaves and attempts to secure their freedom. Even Tom, though male and physically powerful, becomes, in Stowe's paradigm, a feminine-identified Christ figure who prioritizes relationships with the divine and other human beings over his own freedom, who exemplifies nurture and gentleness, who unashamedly weeps, and who embraces weakness over strength to the point of death to secure the "salvation," physical and spiritual, of others.

Tom's identification with the maternal is intentional: Stowe crafted her best-selling novel with the goal of showing "how Jesus Christ . . . has still a mother's love for the poor and lowly" (C. E. Stowe, *Life* 154), and in doing so, she was not the first to feminize the nature of Christian divinity. . . .

Medieval mystics as early as the twelfth century but even more frequently during the two centuries that followed wrote of the second person of the trinity as a mother.[9] This trend reaches its culmination in the fourteenth-century female mystic Julian of Norwich, who insists, in one of many such passages: "The Saviour himself is our Mother for we are forever being born of him and shall never be delivered" and "The human mother will suckle her child with her milk, but our beloved mother, Jesus, feeds us with himself" (164). Relative to the conservatism of her culture, Stowe's endowing her novel's male and female Christ figures with maternal attributes certainly appears radical; however, given her particularly thorough knowledge of Hebrew and Christian scriptures, many of which celebrate the mothering of God, her technique becomes, perhaps, less surprising.[10]

Even Stowe's secondary characters who portray negative maternal images do so to underscore the centrality of motherhood: the slave Prue, for example, has become an alcoholic precisely *because* of being forced to hear her infant wail as it starved to death; Northern abolitionist Ophelia, who is frightened to touch black skin, becomes a sympathetic character only once she begins to function as priest and parent toward Topsy; Cassy's redemption begins when she is able to act as a mother and protector toward Emmeline, a kind of black Evangeline; and Marie's self-absorbed obsessions become substantially more monstrous, as Stowe has framed it, when juxtaposed with the mother of Christ, from which her name derives, and contrasted with the self-sacrificial redemptive power of the book's other mothers. Plantation-romance and anti-Uncle Tom writers also attempt to display mother figures as the salvation for personal and societal ills—yet with very different results.

Notes

9. See particularly Bynum, *Jesus as Mother*, but also Lerner, *Creation*, and Wacker.

10. Attending a graduate seminar with Elizabeth Ammons and later reading her essays on Stowe first led me to consider what Ammons calls "the odd equation of mothers/Eva/Tom, an equation which, if followed through to its logical conclusion, argues the radical substitution of feminine and maternal for masculine values" ("Heroines" 163). From there, I began making connections with feminist theology's assertions and examining the rebuttals to Stowe for similar theological themes.

SARAH MEER ON ASPECTS OF MINSTRELSY IN *UNCLE TOM'S CABIN*

The first reviews of *Uncle Tom's Cabin* lingered not only over the weepy deathbeds of Eva and Uncle Tom but also over comic aspects of the novel. Unlike later critics, nineteenth-century observers were particularly struck by the humor in the book, which was attested to by reviewers from both the North and the South in the United States as well as in Britain. . . .

The emphases on comedy, on black life, and on dialogue and "negro-English" and the fascination with Topsy's "impishness" single out aspects of *Uncle Tom's Cabin* that were also the attributes audiences claimed to enjoy in blackface entertainment. More pointedly, many reviews explicitly invoked the minstrel show as a comparison. . . .

By the time Stowe began her book blackface had permeated U.S. culture, and both its icons and versions of its acts could be found everywhere. . . . Moreover, minstrel show songs were available as sheet music, its jokes and sketches were published in books, and devotees admiringly repeated its material on the streets. . . .

Minstrel show set pieces, which themselves contained a number of possible ways of relating to the characters on the stage, were converted in Stowe's novel into powerful devices for reallocating sympathy. One tradition Stowe reworked with particular subtlety, the dialogues between the end man and the interlocutor, worked in the minstrel show both to dramatize class tension and to supplant conflict with the ludicrous and nonsensical. Class is crucial in Stowe's writing—her sentimental vision of matriarchal power is implicitly middle class. However, the end man–interlocutor scenes in the minstrel show are highly ambivalent about precisely the social world *Uncle Tom* valorizes, approaching it with a fine balance of mockery and aspiration. By incorporating such scenes into her novel, even in an adapted form, Stowe complicated its class appeal, positing an ironic distance from bourgeois values as well as an identification with them. Like the members of minstrel show audiences, *Uncle Tom's* readers inhabit several positions at once.

In the minstrel show the debates between the end man and the interlocutor took place in the first act, between performers sitting in a semicircle on the stage. The end men, who wore rags and spoke with "black" accents, bantered with the immaculately suited interlocutor, whose diction was not only middle class but prone to exaggeratedly complex and Latinate phrasing. As they traded remarks, the end men frequently misunderstood and vulgarized the interlocutor's point, while the interlocutor struggled vainly to assert the respectable, or standard English, interpretation of his utterance. Often he took on specific roles, imitating reformers, preachers, or academics, all those "who from the vantage point of superior class, education, or morality, presumed to lecture the mob."[46] As with most blackface, the weight of the comedy varied in different performances, but often the jibes were not only directed at "black" misuse of language but also worked to undercut the genteel airs of the interlocutor. What appeared to be and sometimes was also a racist attack on black speakers was also a dig at the standardizing and ornate language of the upper echelons.

These exchanges are echoed a number of times in *Uncle Tom's Cabin*, and Stowe not only reproduced the double-edged quality of the stage satire but also extended and complicated its possibilities. In an early scene that dramatizes the way positions can be simultaneously censored and celebrated in the novel, Mrs. Shelby is instructing Sam to help the slave catcher go after Eliza and her child. She is also signaling, less overtly, that she would rather be helping them get away. In the midst of her doublespeak, Mrs. Shelby herself is distracted by Sam's propensity for taking his Maker's name in vain. What ensues could be an end man–interlocutor exchange, during which Mrs. Shelby takes on the interlocutor role, ordering, teaching, and reforming, and Sam becomes the end man, disrupting, mocking, and blaspheming:

> "Why have you been loitering so, Sam? I sent Andy to tell you to hurry."
>
> "Lord bless you, Missis!" said Sam, "horses won't be cotched all in a mimit; they'd done clared out way down to the south pasture, and the Lord knows whar!"
>
> "Sam, how often must I tell you not to say 'Lord bless you, and the Lord knows,' and such things? It's wicked."
>
> "O, Lord bless my soul! I done forgot, Missis! I won't say nothing of the sort no more."
>
> "Why, Sam, you just have said it again."
>
> "Did I? O, Lord! I mean—I didn't go fur to say it."
>
> "You must be *careful* Sam."
>
> "Just let me get my breath, Missis, and I'll start fair. I'll be berry careful."
>
> "Well, Sam, you are to go with Mr. Haley, to show him the road, and help him. Be careful of the horses, Sam; you know Jerry was a little lame last week; *don't ride them too fast*." (UTC 39–40)[47]

Mrs. Shelby, as interlocutor, instructs Sam in correct linguistic practice and demands reverent comportment. Persistently transgressing, Sam achieves the end man's dance between ignorance and mockery in his counterproductive attempts to stop blaspheming. He conceals a hint of cheek in a hopeless attempt to conform. Yet in the larger context of the slave-catching chapters, this scene's class configurations are more subtle and more surprising than the minstrel duality would suggest.

Sam has been tipped off that Mrs. Shelby privately hopes that the fugitives will get away. His blasphemies, which necessitate Mrs. Shelby's reprimands and instruction, cause delay, which buys time for Eliza and Harry. Although Sam's language appears to challenge Mrs. Shelby and to set up confrontation, its time-consuming provocation also works in her interest, increasing the chances that the runaways will escape. Thus, the interval produced by this end man–interlocutor role play represents both class conflict and also a cross-class alliance. The end man and the interlocutor's combat is also a conspiracy. To mix matters up still further, Haley, the white slave catcher, has been established in the opening scenes of the novel as deeply uncouth, in speech as in all else, While Sam's slips and errors work in alignment with Mrs. Shelby's prim disapproval, their opponent is "coarse," "low," and "overdressed." White gentility is in league with black vulgarity against white "coarseness": Sam's exclamations, however sacrilegious themselves, are arraigned against the "profane" slave trader (*UTC*, 1).

This alliance is still in operation when Sam induces Haley's horse to unseat his owner, "accidently" waves his palm leaf in its eyes, and unleashes "a miscellaneous scene of confusion" while horses bolt, dogs bark, and Mike, Mose, Mandy, and Fanny "raced, clapped hands, whooped, and shouted, with outrageous officiousness and untiring zeal" (*UTC*, 41). This could be minstrel show slapstick; as on the stage, it could also represent a disruption of the industrial work ethic, enabling first-generation urban audiences to laugh with as much as at black characters who would rather dance and go hunting than put in long hours of labor.[48] Yet if this scene similarly enshrines both an apparent critique of black shiftlessness and a delight in it, it differs from the minstrel show in suggesting the genteel sanction of Mrs. Shelby. Stowe includes her middle-class forces of discipline and order in the novel; unlike those of the stage interlocutors, they are often explicitly feminine, and here they are also in league with blackface chaos.

Uncle Tom's Cabin thus adapts the minstrel show's capacity, in Dale Cockrell's words, "to ridicule both up and down the social ladder simultaneously," reapplying it with significant adjustments to class and gender.[49] It is not just ridicule that moves in this scene but also sympathy, and it is not a straightforward journey. Whether the reader identifies most with Sam's linguistic license or with Mrs. Shelby's corrective impulse, procrastination brings the two into collusion. Social position here cannot be marked out simply as rungs on a ladder, and sympathy must chart a path complicated enough to encompass both mistress and slave without visiting the lower-class white.

The oscillating satire and sympathy of the end man–interlocutor dialogues demonstrate the way in which comically uneducated, self-serving, or cowardly characters can also serve to make digs at white slave-owning society. If the novel is inspected for blackface dualities, some of its most demeaning portraits can be found at points where sentiment has the greatest force. The sentimental also amplifies the comedy, adding another layer of meaning to blackface wordplay that is often an antislavery point. On the stage, parodies of sermons, lectures, and stump speeches evinced the same pattern of overt mockery of (and discreet pleasure in) linguistic anarchy as the end man dialogues, and the novel also adapted this blackface convention.

Notes

46. Zanger, "The Minstrel Show," 34. On the structure of the minstrel show and on this part of the act see Toll, *Blacking Up*, 52–57.

47. I would not dispute Davis's argument that Sam's "hilarious fun-loving semi-roguery" here is "kin" to that of servant figures in Walter Scott and his disciples, James Fenimore Cooper and William Gilmore Simms, but the dialectical structure of this dialogue is more specifically derived from the stage ("Mrs. Stowe's Characters-in-Situations," 114).

48. See Roediger, *The Wages of Whiteness*, 61–81; also Saxton, *The Rise and Fall of the White Republic*, 165–82. Lhamon also comments on the blackface aspects of Topsy's "raising Cain" (*Raising Cain*, 144).

49. Cockrell, *Demons of Disorder*, 94.

HENRY LOUIS GATES, JR. REEVALUATES *UNCLE TOM'S CABIN*

Coming to *Uncle Tom's Cabin* again in middle age, . . . I am struck by two things: the extent to which Harriet Beecher Stowe's forceful political voice is grounded in home and family and how much of the novel's sentimentality fails to mask its polymorphous sexual energy. . . .

The fact of the novel's domesticity shouldn't really be a surprise. The title of the book refers to a home (or at least a rude shelter). Should we be surprised that we ignored the issue of house and home during a radically political time when . . . the Student Nonviolent Coordinating Committee was asking, incredibly, in its position paper on Black Power: "Who is the real villain—Uncle Tom or Simon Legree?"[2] We had seen the enemy, and the enemy was, if not us, than at least one of us. . . .

Stowe's novel is thoroughly preoccupied with marriages—broken-up marriages, failed marriages, fatalistic and tired marriages; bittersweet, evergreen, surprisingly emotional marriages; hasty, postponed, "if-only" marriages; in-name-only, bitter, clinging, and doomed marriages. . . .

It would be easy to dismiss the topic of marriage as a kind of contrapuntal melody, a leitmotif about "the marriage bonds" that either softens or puts in stark relief the unyielding bonds of slavery, but this would be to undervalue the complexity of Stowe's rhetorical strategy. . . .

Stowe uses the metonym of the cabin—Tom's doomed marital home—to remove the question of slavery from the male discourse of Jeffersonian individualism, which had not had much success in ending slavery by 1852, and to resituate it squarely in the heart of the family circle. By depicting Uncle Tom and George Harris not as perfect men but as perfect *husbands*—and, while doing so, implicitly provoking her female readers to ask if their own husbands embodied the ideal of Christian decency—Stowe probably managed to unsettle tens of thousands of marriages that had not had, and would never have, any *direct* connection to slavery. . . .

I would like to think that a truly rational, intellectually honest human being could not help but oppose slavery, though part of me understood that the issue is far more complex than that, especially given slavery's history in black Africa, and even black-on-black slavery in the antebellum South. This aside, what other reason could there be to oppose slavery besides the obvious rational and ethical grounds? What did marriage possibly have to do with it?

Stowe's great claim was that men might embrace antislavery politics because their wives expected better of them. Judging by the public's unprecedented, overwhelming response to the novel, she was surely on to something. What choice did men have if American women wanted their lovers to be as passionate and ambitious as George Harris, as loyal and uncomplaining as Senator Bird, as pious and brawny as John Van Trompe ("a great, tall bristling Orson of a fellow, full six feet and some inches in his stockings"), and as moral and steadfast as dear old Uncle Tom? . . .

Let us begin with Uncle Tom's marital status, a subject that has long intrigued Stowe scholars. In the early part of the story, on the Shelby plantation, Uncle Tom's relationship with Aunt Chloe is implied but never explicitly stated. The reader is meant to understand that Tom and Chloe are married and have three children, but they never speak about their passion for each other. Stowe represents Tom as a devoted—even doting—father, but not as a lover. . . . The "snowy spread" that covers the public bed is meant to signify the neatness and cleanliness of these exceptional slaves, refuting the stereotype of their lack of respectability.

Conception between Tom and Chloe could well be as immaculate as the bedspread. For these two there is none of the sexual chemistry that obtains between the other married couples: the nearly white George and Eliza, Senator and Mrs. Bird, and the blushing Quaker newlyweds. This lack is perhaps meant to signify the perilous and legally fragile nature of slave "marriage." But one no doubt unintended effect of this striking absence is to suggest that pure black slaves like Tom and Chloe are not capable of sublime feelings, reinforcing stereotypes of their privileging of the physical and quotidian over the metaphysical, as it were. The "sublime mystery" in the cabin is Chloe's corn cake recipe.

The problem with Uncle Tom and Chloe's sexuality is that it is depicted, if that is the right word, in the passive voice, as it were. Whereas the sexuality of Eliza and George is a burning, active passion—one even sanctioned, extraordinarily, by an elaborate wedding ceremony hosted by their mistress in the Big House—Tom and Chloe's is a highly mediated passion, somnolent almost, buried deep under Aunt Chloe's apron and Tom's gray, balding head. In fact, so at odds are their sobriquets of "Uncle" and "Aunt" with the young ages of their children that trying to imagine Tom and Chloe making love is a bit like being forced to imagine your parents (or worse, your grandparents) procreating with abandon in the dark recesses of the cabin. Just where did those babies of Chloe's come from? Given her physical description and social status among the neighbors, we can't help but think of her as old and venerable—which, given the youth of her children, evokes the image of a black Sarah, conceiving in her old age.

Stowe works hard to ensure that Tom leaves his cabin a man free from domestic bonds. Her text renders Tom's sexuality in such an ambivalent manner, chaining Tom's potency, I believe, to enable an entirely safe level of intimacy between Tom and Eva that would have been scandalous otherwise. The fact of the matter—which, curiously enough, has not escaped the attention of generations of the novel's illustrators—is that Tom leaves his home and almost immediately becomes involved with a young blonde.

It never occurred to me to think of the novel this way until the early 1980s. . . .

Had I missed something in the novel? Was my middle-school edition expurgated? Had I neglected to find the deeper meaning inherent in this literary work's formal and rhetorical strategies, as we had been taught to do in eighth-grade English class? What is worse, had my hero, James Baldwin, himself missed the subtext of dripping sexuality in the novel's portrayal of Tom and Eva's first embrace, when he, "broad-chested, strong-armed . . . caught her in his arms, and, swimming with her to the boat-side, handed her up" (pp. 157–58)?

Tom and Little Eva "meet cute," as they say in Hollywood. He is poor, she is rich; after he saves her life on the cruise ship, she brings him home with her; they spend long, halcyon days together, holding hands and walking; she becomes sick and dies, and he is cast out when the only remaining person who could protect him dies as well. . . .

Stowe all but dares the reader to see something untoward in the obsessive closeness of Uncle Tom and Little Eva. While their relationship is most certainly not sexual, it is undoubtedly—and remarkably—physical: Tom and Eva touch, kiss, hold hands, hold each other closely. It is an unfolding flaunting of the taboo of "amalgamation," of cross-racial sexual intimacy. Judging from the popular and scandalous images of Tom with nubile white women and girls that have outlived the book's canonical status in the classroom, Mrs. Stowe was not entirely successful in her attempt to neuter Tom. . . .

Stowe's sentimental form enabled her story's sexual content. The number of such images that proliferated after the publication of *Uncle Tom's Cabin* demonstrates the public recognition that a universe of sex lay submerged beneath the surface of her novel. . . . The vulgar, racist, sexualized images of black men—thick lipped, lascivious—groping at white women were a visceral response to what racists recognized to be the subversive message concealed not only in the proximity of the cabin and the Big House but also in the intimacy between Eva and Tom. Amalgamation was about sex. Race mingling was about sex. Abolition was about sex, because slavery, in part, was about unbridled, unregulated sex, always potentially available in the relation between master and slave.

Sentimentality masks sexuality by focusing attention on the outside of the body—tears, sighs, blushes—such that the body itself recedes from focus. Sentimentalism is concerned with the space between a body and the eyes watching it. Still, the body is always present, along with its potential for consummation. After all, the picture of Uncle Tom's strong arms around Little Eva's little white waist is the central image of the entire middle section of the book. While sentimentality attempted to function to mask or repress sexuality, it also inadvertently functioned to draw attention to it.

Note

2. "Student Nonviolent Coordinating Committee Position Paper: The Basis of Black Power"; see http://www3.iath.virginia.edu.sixties/HTML_docs/Resources/Primary/Manifestos/SNCC_black_power.html

Works by Harriet Beecher Stowe

Primary Geography for Children (with Catherine Beecher), 1833.

A New England Sketch, 1834.

The Mayflower; or, Sketches of Scenes and Characters among the Descendants of the Pilgrims, 1843.

Uncle Tom's Cabin; or, Life among the Lowly, 1852. 2 vols.

Earthly Care, a Heavenly Discipline, 1852.

The Two Altars; or, Two Pictures in One, 1852.

History of the Edmondson Family, c. 1852.

A Key to Uncle Tom's Cabin: Presenting the Original Facts and Documents upon Which the Story Is Founded, 1853, 1854.

Uncle Sam's Emancipation; Earthly Care, a Heavenly Discipline; and Other Sketches, 1853.

The Coral King, 1853.

Letter to the Ladies' New Anti-Slavery Society of Glasgow, c. 1853.

Sunny Memories of Foreign Lands, 1854. 2 vols.

Notice of the Boston Anti-Slavery Bazaar, c. 1854.

First Geography for Children, 1855.

The May Flower and Miscellaneous Writings, 1855.

The Christian Slave, 1855.

What Should We Do without the Bible?, c. 1855.

Dred: A Tale of the Great Dismal Swamp, 1856. 2 vols.

Mrs. H. B. Stowe on Dr. Monod and the American Tract Society, Considered in Relation to American Slavery, 1858.

My Expectation, 1858.

My Strength, 1858.

Things That Cannot Be Shaken, 1858.

Strong Consolation; or, God a Refuge and Strength, 1858.

A Word to the Sorrowful, 1858.

Our Charley, and What to Do with Him, 1858.

Harriet Beecher Stowe on the American Board of Commissioners for Foreign Missions, c. 1858.

The Minister's Wooing, 1859.

The Pearl of Orr's Island: A Story of the Coast of Maine, 1862.

Agnes of Sorrento, 1862.

A Reply to The Affectionate and Christian Address of Many Thousands of Women of Great Britain and Ireland, to Their Sisters, the Women of the United States: In Behalf of Many Thousands of American Women, 1863.

Primitive Christian Experience, c. 1863.

The Ravages of a Carpet, c. 1864.

House and Home Papers, 1865.

Stories about Our Dogs, 1865.

Little Foxes, 1866.

Religious Poems, 1867.

The Daisy's First Winter and Other Stories, 1867.

Queer Little People, 1867.

The Chimney-Corner, 1868.

Men of Our Times; or, Leading Patriots of the Day, 1868.

Oldtown Folks, 1869.

The American Woman's Home; or, Principles of Domestic Science (with Catherine E. Beecher), 1869, 1870 (as *Principles of Domestic Science*) and 1874 (as *The New Housekeeper's Manual*).

Lady Byron Vindicated: A History of the Byron Controversy from Its Beginning in 1816 to the Present Time, 1870.

Little Pussy Willow, 1870.

Pink and White Tyranny: A Society Novel, 1871.

My Wife and I; or, Harry Henderson's History, 1871.

Have You Seen It? Letter from Mrs. Stowe to Miss Kate Reignolds, c. 1871.

Sam Lawson's Oldtown Fireside Stories, 1872.

"*He's Coming To-morrow*," c. 1872.

Palmetto-Leaves, 1873.

Woman in Sacred History, 1873.

We and Our Neighbors; or, The Records of an Unfashionable Street, 1875.

Betty Bright Idea, 1876.

Footsteps of the Master, 1877.

Poganuc People: Their Loves and Lives, 1878.

A Dog's Mission; or, The Story of the Old Avery House, and Other Stories, 1881.

Flowers and Fruit from the Writings of Harriet Beecher Stowe, ed. Abbie H. Fairfield, 1888.

Dialogues and Scenes from the Writings of Harriet Beecher Stowe, ed. Emily Weaver, 1889.

Life of Harriet Beecher Stowe Compiled from Her Letters and Journals, ed. Charles Edward Stowe, 1889.

Writings, 1896. 16 vols.

Life and Letters, ed. Annie Fields, 1897.

Collected Poems, ed. John Michael Moran, Jr., 1967.

Regional Sketches: New England and Florida, ed. John R. Adams. 1972.

Uncle Tom's Cabin; *The Minister's Wooing*; *Oldtown Folks*, 1982.

Annotated Bibliography

Ammons, Elizabeth, ed. *Uncle Tom's Cabin: Harriet Beecher Stowe*, Norton Critical Edition. New York: W. W. Norton & Company, 1994.

Following the annotated text of Stowe's novel are three sections, the first devoted to presenting documents related to slavery, abolition, and Southern culture; the second divided between early reviews and receptions of the novel and a sampling of recent criticism informed by the numerous controversies generated by the book and its popular and critical reception. A chronology of Stowe's life and a selected bibliography are also included. This volume is an excellent introduction to *Uncle Tom's Cabin* and the numerous debates it has generated, but it contains as well valuable information for the advanced reader.

Ammons, Elizabeth, and Susan Belasco, eds. *Approaches to Teaching Stowe's "Uncle Tom's Cabin."* New York: Modern Language Association of America, 2000.

The contents of the Modern Language Association Approaches to Teaching series are consistently well researched and insightful. Teaching and reading *Uncle Tom's Cabin* presents unusual difficulties beginning with the volatility of discussions about race introduced in classrooms of diverse students. There is also the issue of the author's unflagging appeal to the reader's emotions—and whether this strategy reduces the novel to mere sentimentality, exempting it from serious critical consideration. In addition to discussions of ways to teach the novel in diverse contexts, there is a substantial listing of resource materials.

Gates, Henry Louis, Jr., and Hollis Robbins, eds. *The Annotated "Uncle Tom's Cabin."* New York: W. W. Norton & Company, 2007.

This recently published oversized volume is designed for new readers of *Uncle Tom's Cabin* as well as advanced students and scholars. In the introduction, Henry Louis Gates, Jr. offers a reevaluation of the novel, contrasting the views he held during the years of Black Power activism with more current considerations. James Baldwin's famous harsh criticism of Harriet Beecher Stowe and the novel is discussed along with commentary about aspects of the novel both critics may have overlooked. In addition to the extensive notes in the margins of the text itself are dozens of exceptionally interesting illustrations. These include: wood engravings of old illustrations from the book itself and the pamphlets and publicity for it; examples of different covers used for the numerous editions of the novel; color lithographs inspired by scenes and characters; strips from the Classics Illustrated Comic Books series on *Uncle Tom's Cabin*; and numerous random cartoons and jokes, including "Condoleezza Rice Crossing the Ice," a depiction of the current secretary of state in the guise of Eliza fleeing the slave trader and hostile dogs named "Kerry," "Boxer," and "Biden."

Gossett, Thomas F. *"Uncle Tom's Cabin" and American Culture*. Dallas: Southern Methodist University Press, 1985.

Thomas Gossett looks at *Uncle Tom's Cabin* as a major cultural phenomenon. This substantial work functions as a kind of biography of Stowe's novel: its antecedents; its history; its separate reception in the North, South, Great Britain, and Europe; its effect on antislavery legislation; the proliferation of anti-Tom novels; and its function as an index of racism in the United States. The early chapters focus on Stowe's life, the Beecher family history, abolition, and the author's ideas about race. Sixteen illustrations—old photographs and drawings from the novel and its times—are included. Of special interest are three different drawings of Eliza's escape over the ice-jammed Ohio River and the cover of a Russian edition of the novel.

Jordan-Lake, Joy. *Whitewashing "Uncle Tom's Cabin": Nineteenth-Century Woman Novelists Respond to Stowe*. Nashville: Vanderbilt University Press, 2005.

Among the most interesting reactions to Stowe's novel was the arrival on the Southern literary scene of numerous anti-Uncle Tom novels written by women in rebuttal. Jordan-Lake examines how these women writers defended slavery and the Southern way of life by concocting a "theology of whiteness" in their own novels. She discusses in detail some of these novels in which the Christian God is viewed as ordaining and condoning the practice of slavery out of compassion for the Negro race. This view turns on the assumption of black inferiority and helplessness which the author finds essentially groundless; much of the book is taken up in debunking it from theological and cultural perspectives. The author also examines the social consequences of one group securing its economic strengths at the expense of another.

Kohn, Denise, Sarah Meer, and Emily B. Todd, eds. *Transatlantic Stowe: Harriet Beecher Stowe and European Culture*. Iowa City: University of Iowa Press, 2006.

Uncle Tom's Cabin brought international fame to Stowe; the novel was quickly translated in several languages. Appearing at a time when American authors had little international standing, Stowe came to represent the emergence of a distinctly American literature. The editors present essays covering many features of this transatlantic phenomenon, including the unexpected ways that "*Uncle Tom's Cabin* fractured relationships as well as [forged] them," (p. xxiii).

Lowance, Mason I., Jr., Ellen E. Westbrook, R. C. DeProspo, eds. *The Stowe Debate: Rhetorical Strategies in "Uncle Tom's Cabin."* Amherst: The University of Massachusetts Press, 1994.

This collection of essays is organized around three areas of controversy generated by Stowe and her novel: the pro- and antislavery debate; the critical debate; and contemporary conversations about how to read and understand the novel. Contributors to the volume address questions of language, rhetoric, and nineteenth- and twentieth-century discourses about race and domesticity.

Meer, Sarah. *Uncle Tom Mania: Slavery, Minstrelsy & Transatlantic Culture in the 1850s*. Athens: The University of Georgia Press, 2005.

"Tom-Mania" is a British term for the phenomenal transatlantic response that Stowe's novel generated in the first years following publication. Meer begins by observing that many of the novel's scenes are simultaneously comic and sad with attributes similar to minstrel theatrics. Specifically, Meer argues that Stowe's use of features associated with minstrelsy helped create the furor over the book. After reviewing the history and ramifications of minstrelsy in the United States, the author discusses the novel's early reception in the country, its adaptation in Britain, and American responses to these British adaptations, tracing through all versions the ambiguities and subtleties that minstrelsy techniques made possible for a wide readership. Meer examines some of the anti-Tom texts and devotes one chapter to *Dred*, Stowe's less well-known antislavery novel. One aim of her study is to suggest "how a definitive meaning for the novel has remained for so long tantalizing and always elusive" (p. 17).

Noble, Marianne. *The Masochistic Pleasures of Sentimental Literature*. Princeton: Princeton University Press, 2000.

In this examination of sentimental literature, female masochism, and erotic suffering, Noble cites Stowe's *Uncle Tom's Cabin* as the novel that displays "the complications of nineteenth-century woman's exploitation of sentimental masochism for power and pleasure [most] vividly . . ." (p. 126). She devotes a chapter to reading Stowe in this context. Noble identifies her book as a challenge to recent feminist attitudes about sentimentalism, "which have argued that the pleasures the genre offered female readers lay not in its celebration of the pleasures of submission but in its assertion of female desires for autonomy and agency" (p. 5).

Scott, John Anthony. *Woman Against Slavery: The Story of Harriet Beecher Stowe*. New York: Thomas Crowell Company, 1978.

This biography of Stowe examines those aspects of her life that led to her writing the world's most famous antislavery novel. Scott notes the damage done to both the novel and to black people by the outbreak of traveling "Tom shows" that misrepresented the slaves and their stories. He writes in hope of contributing to a reassessment of the novel. He helpfully includes discussions of American history in the years leading up to the novel's publication—the threat of secession made by the South and the compromises worked out in the U.S. Congress. Scott's study is a good example of work done in praise of Stowe before it became unavoidable to examine evidence of the author's own racism.

Weinstein, Cindy. *The Cambridge Companion to Harriet Beecher Stowe*. Cambridge: Cambridge University Press, 2004.

Like many entries in the Cambridge Companion series, this edition on Harriet Beecher Stowe begins with a premise that all contributors respond to from their diverse perspectives. In her introduction, Cindy Weinstein takes off from the fabled exchange between Abraham Lincoln and Harriet Beecher Stowe in which the president paid tribute to the power of Stowe's words to change history. Some of the questions addressed focus on the power of words to influence nations and individuals. Also addressed is the contradiction inherent in the novel, namely, its progressive view of abolishing the practice of slavery while advocating in the place of integration the colonization of freed slaves in the African state of Liberia. A chronology and twelve essays are offered.

Contributors

Harold Bloom is Sterling Professor of the Humanities at Yale University. He is the author of 30 books, including *Shelley's Mythmaking*, *The Visionary Company*, *Blake's Apocalypse*, *Yeats*, *A Map of Misreading*, *Kabbalah and Criticism*, *Agon: Toward a Theory of Revisionism*, *The American Religion*, *The Western Canon*, and *Omens of Millennium: The Gnosis of Angels, Dreams, and Resurrection*. *The Anxiety of Influence* sets forth Professor Bloom's provocative theory of the literary relationships between the great writers and their predecessors. His most recent books include *Shakespeare: The Invention of the Human*, a 1998 National Book Award finalist, *How to Read and Why*, *Genius: A Mosaic of One Hundred Exemplary Creative Minds*, *Hamlet: Poem Unlimited*, *Where Shall Wisdom Be Found?*, and *Jesus and Yahweh: The Names Divine*. In 1999, Professor Bloom received the prestigious American Academy of Arts and Letters Gold Medal for Criticism. He has also received the International Prize of Catalonia, the Alfonso Reyes Prize of Mexico, and the Hans Christian Andersen Bicentennial Prize of Denmark.

Solomon Northup was a slave.

William Wells Brown was an ex-slave and abolitionist.

James Baldwin (1924–1987) is best known for *Notes of a Native Son* (1955), his autobiographical account of struggling against poverty, discrimination, and hatred to emerge as an articulate spokesman for his generation. He also wrote *Nobody Knows My Name* (1961) and *The Evidence of Things Not Seen* (1985).

Jane P. Tompkins is the author of *Sensational Designs: The Cultural Work of American Fiction, 1790–1860* (1985).

Thomas F. Gossett is the author of the important work on racism, *Race: The History of an Idea in America* (1963).

Robert S. Levine is the author of *Martin Delany, Frederick Douglass, and the Politics of Representative Identity* (1997).

Elizabeth Ammons is professor of English and American studies at Tufts. She is the editor of *Critical Essays on Harriet Beecher Stowe* (1980) and the Norton Critical Edition of Edith Wharton's *House of Mirth* and Harriet Beecher Stowe's *Uncle Tom's Cabin*.

Marianne Noble's essay, "'An Ecstasy of Apprehension': The Gothic Pleasures of Sentimental Fiction," is included in *American Gothic: New Interventions in a National Narrative* (1998).

Samuel Otter teaches English at the University of California at Berkeley. In 1999 he published *Melville's Anatomies*.

Cindy Weinstein teaches literature at the California Institute of Technology. In 1995 she published *The Literature of Labor and the Labors of Literature: Allegory in Nineteenth-Century American Literature*.

Joy Jordan-Lake taught English at Baylor University and Belmont University in Nashville. She has graduate degrees in both literature and theology.

Sarah Meer is university lecturer in English at the University of Cambridge and a fellow of Selwyn College.

Henry Louis Gates, Jr. is director of the W.E.B. Du Bois Institute and professor of humanities at Harvard. Gates was recently appointed to a newly endowed chair at Harvard—the Alphonse Fletcher Jr. University Professorship—in African and African American research. He is popularly known as the scholar who has done genealogical research with prominent Americans such as Colin Powell, Whoopi Goldberg, and Oprah Winfrey.

Acknowledgments

Solomon Northup, "A Slave Auction Described by a Slave, 1841," from *Uncle Tom's Cabin*, © 1994 by W. W. Norton & Company, Inc.

William Wells Brown, "Another Kidnapping, 1844," from *Uncle Tom's Cabin*, © 1994 by W. W. Norton & Company, Inc.

"Anonymous [Review of *Uncle Tom's Cabin*]," from *Uncle Tom's Cabin*, © 1994 by W. W. Norton & Company, Inc.

From *Notes of a Native Son* by James Baldwin. Copyright © 1955, renewed 1983, by James Baldwin. Reprinted by permission of Beacon Press, Boston.

Excerpts from Jane Tompkins, *Sensational Designs: The Cultural Work of American Fiction, 1790–1860*. New York: Oxford University Press, 1985. Reprinted with permission.

Epilogue by Thomas F. Gossett. From *Uncle Tom's Cabin and American Culture*: pp. 407, 410–411. © 1985 by Southern Methodist University Press. Reprinted with permission.

From *Martin Delany, Frederick Douglass, and the Politics of Representative Identity* by Robert S. Levine. Copyright © 1997 by the University of North Carolina Press. Used by permission of the publisher. www.uncpress.unc.edu

Reprinted by permission of the Modern Language Association of America from "Empire and Africa" by Elizabeth Ammons. From *Approaches to Teaching Stowe's Uncle Tom's Cabin*, edited by Elizabeth Ammons and Susan Belasco: pp. 74–75. © 2000 by the Modern Language Association of America.

Marianne Nobel, excerpts from "The Ecstasies of Sentimental Wounding in *Uncle Tom's Cabin*" from *The Masochistic*

Pleasures of Sentimental Literature, © 2000 by Princeton University Press.

Excerpts from "Stowe and Race" by Samuel Otter. From *The Cambridge Companion to Harriet Beecher Stowe*, edited by Cindy Weinstein: pp. 18–24, 37. © Cambridge University Press 2004. Reprinted with the permission of Cambridge University Press.

Excerpts from "*Uncle Tom's Cabin* and the South" by Cindy Weinstein. From *The Cambridge Companion to Harriet Beecher Stowe*, edited by Cindy Weinstein: pp. 43–44, 51–52, 55–57. © Cambridge University Press 2004. Reprinted with the permission of Cambridge University Press.

Joy Jordan-Lake, excerpt from "Sanctified by Wealth and Whiteness," from *Whitewashing Uncle Tom's Cabin: Nineteenth-century Women Novelists Respond to Stowe*, © 2005 Vanderbilt University Press.

Excerpts from "Topsy and the End Man" by Sarah Meer. From *Uncle Tom Mania: Slavery, Minstrelsy and Transatlantic Culture in the 1850s*: pp. 21–23, 30–33, 261. © 2005 by the University of Georgia Press. Reprinted with permission.

From *The Annotated Uncle Tom's Cabin* by Harriet Beecher Stowe, edited by Henry Louis Gates Jr. & Hollis Robbins. Copyright © 2007 by Henry Louis Gates Jr. and Hollis Robbins. Used by permission of W. W. Norton & Company, Inc.

Every effort has been made to contact the owners of copyrighted material and secure copyright permission. Articles appearing in this volume generally appear much as they did in their original publication with few or no editorial changes. In some cases, foreign language text has been removed from the original essay. Those interested in locating the original source will find the information cited above.

Index

Characters in literary works are indexed by first name (if any), followed by the name of the work in parentheses.

Y